TAROT

TAROT

The Path to Wisdom

Joseph D'Agostino

SAMUEL WEISER, INC.

York Beach, Maine

First published in 1994 by
Samuel Weiser, Inc.
P. O. Box 612
York Beach, ME 03910-0612

Library of Congress Cataloging-in-Publication Data

D'Agostino, Joseph D.
    Tarot : the path to wisdom / by Joseph
  D'Agostino. -- [New rev. ed.]
        p.   cm.
    1. Tarot.   I. Title.
  BF1879.T2D3   1994
  133.3'2424--dc20   94-36189
                                             CIP
ISBN 0-87728-819-4
CCP

Typeset in 10 point Palatino

Printed in the United States of America

99 98 97 96 95 94
10 9 8 7 6 5 4 3 2 1

The paper used in this publication meets the minimum require-
ments of the American National Standard for Permanence of
Paper for Printed Library Materials Z39.48-1984.

TABLE OF CONTENTS

Part I: The Major Arcana

Part II: Divination

Part III: Introduction to the Qabalah

PREFACE TO THE SECOND EDITION

It is a pleasure to see this volume on tarot symbolism presented in a new edition. Through its years of publication, the fundamental principles inscribed therein, as drawn from my interpretation of the Major Arcana, remain as relevant, vivid and active today as they have been in every age of the tarot's mystical revelations.

These timeless archetypal precepts are embodied deep in the dark realms of the collective unconscious, and form the sure foundation of Eternal Being. When we work with the tarot, we summon these illuminating gems from their abode in that universal treasure-house of images. As these cosmic concepts materialize and thoroughly saturate our thoughts, words, and deeds, the spiritual journey accelerates.

In my experience, I find few methods operative in expanding consciousness that equal the powers of the tarot and its qabalistic counterpart, the Tree of Life. Pondering on the effectiveness of the tarot cards as a meditation tool for enlightenment and transformation, on its astounding accuracy when used as an instrument of divination, it certainly is the royal path of all paths.

—Joseph D. D'Agostino

INTRODUCTION

It is not my intention to discuss the history of the tarot. My goal is to define some of its characteristics in order to make it accessible to its practical use in daily living. The tarot is a deck of seventy-eight cards, twenty-two of which are considered the most important. Numbered from 0 to 21, these unusual picture cards represent that segment of the tarot called the Greater (or Major) Arcana. The remaining 56 cards are subdivided into four sets of symbols identified as Wands, Cups, Swords, and Pentacles. Each suit is numbered from one to ten, and includes four court cards titled King, Queen, Knight, and Page. Combined, these 56 cards form the substance of the Lesser (or Minor) Arcana. Regular playing cards as we know them today were derived from this portion of the Tarot with the exception of the Knight. In the playing card deck, Pentacles became Diamonds, Swords are Spades, Cups are Hearts, and Wands are Clubs.

My interpretation of the tarot is based on the Rider-Waite deck. These esoteric cards are currently available in their original color scheme. Many a writer has speculated on where the tarot cards originated, or who created them, yet no one really knows. For centuries the tarot cards were primarily used for fortunetelling. However, in recent years, it has become widely accepted that these cards can be used for other purposes than divination. The secrets contained in the tarot deck are no longer in the exclusive possession of any select group, and students can discover the wealth of knowledge concerning human behavior that lies concealed behind the various symbols of the 22 cards of the Greater Arcana. These cards display universal signs, basic throughout the world in all ages, common to all beings everywhere, and preserved in what psychology terms the collective unconscious.

The tarot is so rich in symbolism that the patterns of thought it evokes are limitless. Each card follows the other in an orderly sequence, and the series of images have certain mental associations. Experienced readers recommend that a fundamental knowledge of the outer (exoteric) symbolism of the tarot should first be mentally digested in order to use the cards most effectively. Gradual comprehension of the basic language of the tarot enables our consciousness to eventually absorb the deeper significance shown in the cards.

How do we apply the tarot in a practical way? The process will explain itself as we study the cards in numerical order. Each card is a pictorial announcement of some principle or law of life. This "law" exerts an influence on the personality because the natural "language" of the collective unconscious is pictorial symbolism. Psychologists inform us that within the subconscious lies the elements that formulate all that we experience. We also learn that the subconscious can be directed by, and made receptive to, self-conscious suggestion. If we meditate daily on any selected card or combination of cards, the subconscious will be saturated with the fundamental universal creative process. Additionally, continuous meditation will initiate self-analysis, thereby consciously increasing our personal perception of various hidden forces presently active within us.

So if you do your homework and approach tarot practice honestly and intelligently, the tarot will provide a great deal of knowledge about yourself. It will supply you with solutions to help you work out problems successfully, and it will gradually bring beneficial changes in your personality, improving your life and conditions. In the next section, you begin practical study of the tarot by examining the symbols embodied in the twenty-two cards of the Greater Arcana.

PART I
THE MAJOR ARCANA

THE FOOL .

KEY 0
THE FOOL

Before we begin with the interpretation of The Fool, let me outline the daily procedure of practice. Select a period of time each day when you can study the cards without interruption. Twenty to thirty minutes will be sufficient. Focus your attention and examine all the details of the card you study. Focus from right to left, top to bottom, and make a mental note of every symbol—individually and collectively. This ceremony, religiously exercised, will enable you to mentally recall at will any particular detail, or if required, the card in its entirety. Keep a diary and daily record any unusual patterns of thought which may arise in response to a specific card. As you gain a greater understanding of the principles the tarot cards unfold, careful review of this personal record of insights will provoke retrospection and introduce self-analysis.

Key 0, The Fool, is most difficult to define, for here we are confronted with a state of consciousness that is beyond definition. It represents the Total Being; the inner self that religion speaks of; that level of consciousness saints and mystics refer to as Union with God. 0, the number of this card, suggests nothingness, unity without a second, oneness prior to any beginning, the initial and final balance of opposites. We call it Super-Consciousness. Astrologically, the mysterious planetary influence of Uranus is assigned to Key 0, The Fool. Allegorically, in Greek mythology Uranus was an elder god instrumental in producing the first race. The white sun shining in the upper right corner is the Spiritual Sun. It remains forever at forty-five degrees and never reaches its zenith; therefore, it never descends, for the powers of the Self are always at their height and never diminish. It also implies that there is a distinctive relationship between what we call light or solar energy and the substance of this Inner Self.

A youth stands on the top of a mountain peak, symbolizing the completion of a past cycle of activity. However, this youth is restless for new adventures and looks toward greater heights to scale. What he sees is actually an inner vision of the limitless possibilities within himself. The idea that he selects to pursue will be his next goal on the scale of attainment. The magic wand he carries on his shoulder depicts his directed will through which he initiates his course of action. This wand is also a measuring tool, and is painted black, suggesting hidden forces. When we take the right measurement of any given situation or of any particular form, these hidden forces are released, thereby providing us with greater control over portions of ourselves and of our environment. Permanently assimilated into our personality, these manifesting forces are forever available in times of our needs, and at our beckoning.

The pack suspended from the wand is a symbol of the collective unconscious, the memorial storehouse of all our past, present, and future experiences. Its substance is essentially reproductive, and as the golden knob at the end of the wand implies, this substance invariably responds to our self-conscious direction. In The Fool's left hand, he holds a white rose, representing the cultivation and control of the desire nature. Suggested here is activity of ultimate importance, for our predominating desires lead us either into experiences of happiness and success, or misery and failure. The outer garment The Fool wears is the black coat of ignorance, lined with the red cloth of passion, concealing the white robe of perfection. The coat is held closed by a golden girdle consisting of twelve divisions, of which only seven appear. They relate to the seven heavenly planets and the twelve astrological signs of the zodiac.

Before we can remove the coat of ignorance, we must first unfasten the girdle. But the girdle cannot be unfastened until we fully understand the principle of time—a product of the limiting characteristic of personality. The tarot card unfolds an illumination quite essential to practical study, so mull it over carefully. The Eternal Youth is called The Fool, because those of great vision are usually looked upon as being foolish. Then again many a "fool" who speaks is a "windbag," and by association of ideas, the card implies that *pneuma*, spirit, is distinctly related to the most subtle aspect of the air element. Translated into practical application, this brings to our attention that deep rhythmic breathing will not only improve health, but also will improve our power to concentrate and meditate.

You now have a basic awareness of some of the more important symbols and ideas this card exhibits. However, your personal participation in observation and discriminative interpretation is required. There are many other enlightening details for you to discover and recover.

Exercise: If you are frustrated or depressed, look at The Fool. Personal experience will convince you that there is always a positive response.

THE MAGICIAN.

KEY I
THE MAGICIAN

Each tarot card is assigned a number which provides additional information as to its meaning. These numbers symbolically communicate corresponding words, instrumental in expanding our understanding of the basic ideas the cards represent. Wisely, tarot students look upon the knowledge these numbers provide as key words. For example, the number one suggests beginning, inception, initiation, prelude, threshold, and the onset of a new cycle of action.

The Magician, the mercurial master of illusion, personifies what psychologists refer to as objective mind or self-consciousness. Prototyped as masculine, it is this level of consciousness that makes us aware of ourselves and of all that surrounds us. The objective mind—or self-consciousness—is an exclusively human quality, and its essential function is to initiate and direct the course of action of all the creative forces manifesting in both human beings as well as in the universe. The Magician points with his left hand to the subconscious forces below. From this substratum, he draws the necessary material and substance to work with. However, his right hand he holds up high, for originating at the lofty heights of The Fool, he receives the innovative power to formulate and cultivate all that lies at the subconscious levels.

As the universal mediator, The Magician conveys the superconscious objectives as they unfold to the garden below. The posture he holds is probably the most important single aspect of this card. The gesture he exhibits with his left forefinger demonstrates the principle of concentration. This principle endows The Magician with the ability to focus his attention upon a single detail or field of activity. Intelligently implemented, he can observe, analyze, select what he needs, and provide the required adaptations and adjustments he perceives as being beneficial to him. The limiting power of concentration is what expands our consciousness. When we use it constructively we become more human.

The Magician wears the red robe of action, yet he may remove it at will to abstain from all physical activity, and retrospectively meditate on the inner state symbolized by the white robe. The blue-green serpent entwined around his waist relates to the power of transformation, and will be explained when we discuss other cards. Above his head you see the figure eight, the lemniscate, the symbol of continuous creation, renewal, and the affirmation that all opposites are but the expression of a single cause. This distinctly suggests that harmonious integration of personality is our immediate objective. In the garden below, we see the red roses that indicate our active desire nature. There are five roses in bloom because all desire is based in one of the five senses. The four white lilies represent the intellect in passive contemplation of the principles and laws of nature. The knowledge of these principles and laws is derived from the four planes of consciousness—spiritual, mental, astral, and the physical world.

The creative forces The Magician receives from above are always modified by desire and intellect. Therefore, the habitual patterns predominating within his subconscious mind motivate all thought and action. Figuratively, a phallus—the white wand he holds up high in his right hand—speaks of the sublimation of these unconscious forces back into their pristine purity. The ceremonial tools orderly arranged on the table correspond to the four subtle elements we know as fire, water, air, and earth, representing the four phases of creation. Psychologically, the wand (to will) is the initial impulse to create; the cup (to know) is the contemplation upon the unconscious in search of knowledge and enlightenment; the sword (to dare) is the discriminating process of selection and elimination, formulating the creative impulse into its most practical channels of expression; the pentacle (to be silent) is the manifestation of this possessive impulse into a corresponding tangible form.

Exercise: Focus your attention on the details of this card to improve your power of concentration.

THE HIGH PRIESTESS

KEY II
THE HIGH PRIESTESS

The key words suggested by the number two are duplication, duality, sequence, continuation, reflection, reversal, opposition, and reproduction. Symbolically represented as a woman, The High Priestess is what psychology calls subjective mind or subconsciousness. She is that part of our personality shared with all beings below the human level. The High Priestess is the antithesis of The Magician, whose red robe personifies fire and light, and who is actively engaged. She wears a blue garment of water and the night, and sits in a passive state. Like the Moon at her feet, she has no light of her own; rather, she is the receptacle who receives, preserves, and reflects all that has been impressed upon her from above, that is, from superconsciousness (The Fool) and self-consciousness (The Magician). Her fundamental power is memory, and all that is presented in this card refers to this aspect of her power in one manner or another. Actually the entire process and practice of the tarot revolves around this principle of recollection. What these cards unfold to us is the recovery of knowledge we already possess.

The two pillars at her sides are alike in shape and design, but different in color. This represents one of the basic laws of recall, the association of that which is similar or contrasting in nature. We find it also easier to recall those details we most recently recorded, as written on the surface of the scroll she holds in her lap, and by continuous repetition, as the number II and other symbols of dual nature imply. Expounding the Hermetic principle of cause and effect, these two pillars symbolically denote that all we experience is the collective reaction to mental patterns we consciously and unconsciously create. The lotus buds shown on the two pillars reveal that she is the cause of all growth and development. However, the buds are not flowering, acknowledging that she is a virgin, the Eve before her union with Adam, the Veiled Isis of Egyptian mythology. The powers she displays are potential, but for the moment remain latent.

Upon the veil between the pillars we see red pomegranates and green palms, the positive and negative, the male and female, the anticipation of the union of opposites. The connecting veil indicates that this woman is the Uniting Intelligence. It is through the unconscious world that we telepathically communicate with each other, whether we are consciously aware of it or not. Yet I am sure that all of us have had, at some time in our lives, awake or in dreams, an experience of this unusual phenomenon. As the more primitive aspect of personality, the subconscious is the container of all those mysterious and wondrous psychic forces exhibited by true psychics, yogis, and mystics.

Upon her head, The High Priestess wears a horned crown, suggesting the waxing and waning of the Moon. This designation insinuates that rhythm is the crowning principle of her mental activity. The scroll she holds on her lap has inscribed upon it the word *Tora*, meaning "the Law." For written within the scroll is all that we are, and all that we can and will evolve in the future. Her left hand (revealed) speaks of her superficial appearances, and our conscious record of personal impressions. Her right hand (concealed) tells us that the greater part of subconsciousness is always hidden from our view. Yet, she will unveil herself to us for a moment of enlightenment once we understand her character and powers, and learn how to properly approach her.

Exercise: Concentrate upon The High Priestess to improve your memory.

THE EMPRESS.

KEY III
THE EMPRESS

As you have discovered, the past three cards represent superconsciousness, self-consciousness, and subconsciousness. They are the three principal qualities that constitute all human beings. In the world of phenomena, they are of equal stature. Each one depends on the others' function for existence. These first three cards must be looked upon as being in their unaltered state. Those who formulated the tarot presented them singularly, solely for the purpose of studying their nature, and to simplify our comprehension of their specific activities. However, to us they always appear in their compound forms. Beginning with The Empress, and all subsequent cards, these three principles are exhibited in their various proportions and extensions. To what degree we express these proportions and extensions formulates the characteristics of our personality.

The key words the number three suggests are multiplication, germination, productivity, fertility, renewal, augmentation, generation, increase, invention, and unfoldment. In the last card we described The High Priestess as being sterile and passive. Now The Magician, by an act of concentration, focusing his attention upon a portion of her substance, impregnates The High Priestess. The union of opposites takes place and the creative process begins. In Key III, she appears again in guise of The Empress, the pregnant mother in action, expressing herself as creative imagination.

Upon her head The Empress wears a tiara of twelve stars, depicting the twelve signs of the zodiac and her rulership over the universe. She is Mother Nature at work, the basic substance of all creativity. The creative activity of subconsciousness is what psychology terms deductive reasoning. Deductive reasoning is the mental elaboration of a seed idea into its logical conclusion or consequence. However, the subconscious deductive process has no power to analyze or evaluate the seed premise initiated. She will elaborate the false as well as the true, so accordingly, she is the gateway to heaven or to hell. The stars of her tiara are six-pointed hexagrams. They speak of the universal forces manifesting in human personality. These basic human faculties externally appear as memory, will, imagination, desire, the intellect, and the reproductive force. The green wreath binding her yellow hair represents her powers to limit the solar energy of The Fool into special mental forms of expression. The acorns imprinted on her garment are seeds, for she brings forth all the seed possibilities available at the moment. Below we see growing a tract of wheat. Here we observe the fruition of her seeds, our mental images formulated. The white garment reveals that her basic substance remains forever pure and undefiled, regardless of how many forms she may appear in.

The gray stone seat she sits upon is the work of human beings. It is our creative ability to shape her substance into endless variations that brings progress to the world. The Empress wears a necklace of seven pearls, boldly insinuating that her functions play a major role in awakening the seven mysterious psychic centers we have heard yogis speak of. The flowing stream (of the collective unconscious) behind her is another symbol of her continuous association of images. Unaided, she wanders aimlessly, so she depends on self-consciousness to constructively direct her. Within the gray heart at the side of her throne is a symbol of the planet Venus. Venus is the goddess of love, and love is unity. So open your heart to her love. Like the Oneness of The Fool, she is the doorway back to unity—but in a different manner. Contemplation on this enigma will bring you due reward.

Exercise: Meditate on The Empress to constructively improve your powers of imagination.

THE EMPEROR.

KEY IV
THE EMPEROR

Each tarot card is constructed to evoke only positive states of consciousness, therefore daily meditation upon its symbol will stimulate your consciousness with the most creative aspects of your being. Furthermore, by employing these cards in any selected number of combinations, the more complex formulas they preserve can be recovered. However, proficiency in these multiple interpretations demands an adequate comprehension of the basic concepts these twenty-two cards represent.

The key words for the number four suggest order, measurement, system, regulation, classification, arrangement, authority, command, and supervision. With Key IV, The Emperor begins the introduction of the zodiac. The ram heads carved on his throne display the sign of Aries. We collectively share in all the forces the zodiac signs express. However, those of you who have Aries as your Sun sign, rising sign, or Moon sign will discover in this card illuminating insights of special concern, including innate talents, and the unique peculiarities of the Aries temperament. Continuing this practice, as we review subsequent cards, will amply compensate those who diligently examine these astrological correspondences.

The major mental functions assigned to The Emperor are inductive reasoning, and the sense of sight. The Emperor wears the golden crown of the twelve divisions of the zodiac, of which only five are showing. Wearing a crown like The Empress implies his corulership with her over the universe. He is not only her royal consort, but also her complement in the process of creativity. The golden crown, the red garment, the armor of iron, metal of Mars, ruling planet of Aries, indicates that he is another aspect of our self-conscious activity. His performance in observation and inductive reasoning supplies the necessary measuring tools that The Magician requires to expand upon his initial impulse of concentration. The autonomous functions that The Emperor symbolizes are the factors directly engaged in self-analysis. Their activity initiates psychological regression, the reduction of an external form into its primary cause by mentally observing its sequence of events backwards.

Reputed as the Constituting Intelligence, the chief authority, the grand architect of the universe, The Emperor sits on a gray throne proclaiming the powers of human adaptation. At his right arm protrudes a blue undergarment, insinuating that the female aspect of consciousness also plays an important role in his actions. His reasoning faculties are actually an act of recollection, the feminine expression of memory. The light yellow mountains behind him, at the card's left side (the reader's left) are reminiscent of the cold, pure, abstract, as yet infertile, substance of The Fool.

Changing their composition, the mountains at the right side of the picture are a dark yellow, designating that the primordial substance has now been modified by the limiting selective influence of The Magician. In the background below his majesty's throne, course the mighty waters of the collective stream of the unconscious which had its beginning in The High Priestess. The stream is light blue flowing into the picture, and appears in a darker tone as it flows on. Here, the subconscious—in reciprocal response to the modifications formulated above—has comparably altered its contents.

Resembling the symbol of Venus, The Emperor holds in his right hand an Egyptian ankh of life, directing our attention to the generation of images brought forth by The Empress. These images wander aimlessly, and are of no use to him unless he first puts them into some definite order. The particular order in which we have arranged these images dictates our personal interpretation and definition.

The yellow orb and the orange sky represent the Sun exalted in Aries. This solar energy is the element active in the sense of sight. It is how we see ourselves and others that releases the powers of self-consciousness and subconsciousness, either constructively or destructively. The violet cape and the eagle insignia on his left shoulder relate to the planetary forces of Jupiter, astrologically the planet of good fortune and beneficial expansion.* With authority, The Emperor bestows this good fortune upon us, when we apply his powers of reason and sight to their highest degree.

Exercise: Meditate on this card to increase your ability to see things as they really are.

---

*Though the insignia is vague, I perceived with the use of a little imagination, an eagle, therefore, I thought it would be a good opportunity to introduce the symbol of the eagle—as found in The Emperor of the Tarot of Marseilles, an older deck, as well as some other tarot decks—considering that the eagle symbolism has a subtle relationship to The Emperor. Readers may want to read *The Tarot of the Bohemians* by Papus, New York: Samuel Weiser, 1970, pp. 119-121. Reprint available from Wilshire, N. Hollywood, CA.

THE HIEROPHANT

KEY V
THE HIEROPHANT

Most human beings are unaware of the instantaneous minute mental process the tarot cards accurately convey. However, if we are attentive and receptive, the adequate understanding of this vital function will provide an unusual degree of conscious control over creative productivity. Confident, we can then successfully accelerate our objectives. Of course I am assuming that the objectives we select are harmonious in nature.

The key words suggested by number five are mediation, adaptation, adjustment, intervention, will, justice, and reconciliation. Engraved on both sides of the throne, disguised by the author of this deck, is the astrological emblem of the sign of Taurus. Venus is the ruling planet of Taurus, and the Moon is exalted therein; therefore, in this card the powers of The Empress (creative imagination), and The High Priestess (the reproductive faculty of memory), are the most active. The major mental functions assigned to The Hierophant are intuition and the sense of hearing. The Hierophant holds up his right hand bearing the sign of esotericism, signifying hidden knowledge. He is your most inner self, the teacher of the mysteries, The Eternal and Triumphant Intelligence. The knowledge he communicates is an understanding of the principles and laws that govern the universe and our lives. These fundamental ideas are forever present in every age, and always prevail when we sensibly implement them.

The method in which this inner teaching is expounded is what we call intuition. Intuition is the continuation and the evolution of the inductive reasoning process of The Emperor. There cannot be any inner teaching unless the stream of images brought forth by The Empress is first arranged into its proper order by her royal consort. Pursuant to the accurate mental classification of this stream of images, our recovery of the primordial emanations instantly auto-activates the deductive powers of The Hierophant. His unconscious elaborations of these primary forces eventually project into our conscious awareness some principle or law of life. The availability of this ancient wisdom enhances the human solution of personal problems, and universally disseminated, benefits all of us.

The two gray columns on each side of the throne repeat the same ideas we reviewed in Key II, The High Priestess. The acorns inscribed upon each column are the latent archetypal seeds woven and disguised in the multiple images present within the collective unconscious. They remain hidden and undeveloped until unfolded by the intuitive process we have just summarized. The golden staff he holds in his left hand, and the golden crown divided into three layers, establish The Hierophant's rulership over the solar power of light as it flows through the creative, formative, and physical worlds. The upper part of the white pallium he wears over his red robe resembles a circle, suggesting the state of Nothingness we encountered in Key 0, The Fool. Representing the middle pillar of equilibrium, the lower extension of the pallium displays the descent of the spiritual radiant energy into the world of phenomena. Embroidered on the pallium, the equal arm cross, slightly distorted, the calvary cross, the sword cross, and the diamond insignia—which may also be interpreted as the cross of the four elements concealing the inner spirit—describe its course of action in the same manner as the tools we saw on the Magician's table.

On the dais are black and white squares. These squares of opposite colors represent the constant alternation of light and darkness—a product of the principle of rhythm. The two keys at the bottom of the card tell us that The Hierophant unlocks the mysteries of heaven and earth. The bell designs inserted on the two keys speak of the power of sound and the sense of hearing. Two priests kneel before The Hierophant and are listening attentively to what he has to say. The priest on the right, with the white lilies displayed upon his blue robe, personifies intellect. The priest at the left, with red roses on his gray robe, embodies desires. They both wear the yellow yoke of union. Here, the intellect and desire receive their counsel and guidance from the inner teacher. This inner teacher knows the past, present, and the future, and he is in constant communication with you. So, pearl of great price, be silent. Put aside for the moment your emotions, your thoughts, your occupation with insignificant appearances, and listen to his voice. He has a message for you.

Exercise: Meditate on this card to amplify your receptivity to the inner self.

THE LOVERS.

KEY VI
THE LOVERS

The key words suggested by number six are reciprocation, harmony, balance, concord, interchange, response, and integration. The positions of the male and female in the picture are in character with this card's astrological attribution, the twins of the zodiac sign of Gemini. Mercury is the ruling planet of Gemini; therefore, you will find that the self-conscious analytical powers of The Magician are most active in this card. The major functions assigned to The Lovers are the mental performance of discrimination and the sense of smell.

As you look at this card, I am certain that you will be aware that what we have present here is the entire cast of the biblical scene in Genesis—the allegorical story of the creation of man and woman, and of their eventual fall from paradise into sin. Hovering above, under the rays of the Sun of Completeness, is the Archangel Raphael. He has his hands stretched out, symbolizing that he embraces and watches over us—and the entire universe. Raphael is a Hebrew word meaning, "He who heals." The archangel is another aspect of The Hierophant, the God within us, our inner self, who is always present and ready to dispense its healing powers, to assist our need when we seek its help. The white clouds below tell us that the spirit within us is always hidden from the direct view of our self-consciousness. So Adam looks at Eve, and Eve looks at the Angel. It is through the accurate self-conscious scrutiny of the contents and activities of our subconscious, that we become aware of the unfolding powers of the superconscious emanations. Behind Adam grows The Tree of

Life, also identified as The Tree of Consciousness. The tree has twelve branches and the fruit each branch bears is red and yellow threefold flames. These flames of life designate the twelve signs of the zodiac, and the thirty-six subtypes called decanates. This tree speaks of the astrological formula of human creation. Based on the planetary positions at the time of our birth, the unique individualization of our psychological and physical characteristics is due to the collective impact these combined forces of the zodiac manifest.

Behind the woman Eve, we see The Tree of Knowledge of Good and Evil, bearing four red fruit, and a green serpent coiled around its trunk. This tree is a representation of the true and false knowledge that lies within the personal and collective subconscious. The mental function of discrimination follows intuition, because at this point we must carefully examine the elements as they rise from the unconscious into self-conscious awareness. Subsequently, these subliminal observations require that we mentally distinguish between the diverse images of false knowledge based on incompleteness, and the archetypal principles founded upon universal truths. The four fruit on the tree depict the four subine elements of fire, water, air, and earth. These elemental forces are closely associated with faculties of the five human senses. The green serpent, who plays the part of the malicious tempter in Genesis, and in our lives, is also our liberator. The serpent is a portrayal of the reproductive forces of The High Priestess who, as The Empress, generates our images in response to a seed premise initiated on the self-conscious level by The Magician. This mental activity eventually leads us into actions of either wisdom or folly, depending on the quality of knowledge we have incorporated.

In The Lovers, Adam, self-consciousness, and Eve, subconsciousness, enjoy the paradisiacal state.* They are naked, free from all disguise, and in perfect relationship with each other. Can we experience this paradisiacal state of consciousness here on Earth?

---

*In this interpretation, the words of Adam, Eve, man, woman, father, mother, son, and daughter are not to be perceived in physical terms, but rather esoterically, that is, the psychological and inner workings of consciousness, active in all human beings regardless of gender.

In Genesis, God decreed woman to be subjected to man, as her punishment for disobeying his command not to eat the fruit from The Tree of Knowledge of Good and Evil, and for tempting Adam to participate in this abomination. However, in solution, the tarot pictorially expounds that when woman is rightly understood, fully liberated from her subordinating role to man, and returned to her proper place of equal status, then, the same woman that took part in the fall from Paradise will be instrumental in restoring Adam to his throne, and to his dominion over all things in the universe.

Exercise: Meditate on this card to increase your ability of discrimination.

THE CHARIOT.

KEY VII
THE CHARIOT

The key words the number seven suggests are equilibrium, symmetry, rest, poise, safety, security, conquest, mastery, and victory. Inscribed upon the Charioteer's golden belt is the astrological emblem of the zodiac sign of Cancer. The Moon is the ruling planet of Cancer, and the planet Jupiter is exalted therein; therefore the powers of The High Priestess, Memory, and the Law of Rotation, identified with Key X, The Wheel of Fortune, are the most active in this card. The mental functions assigned to The Chariot are will-receptivity, and speech.

Of principal importance, the gray chariot is a moveable body artificially constructed, symbolically representing the limiting, transitory, dependent, vehicle of personality. Described in an ancient text as The Intelligence of the House of Influence, this immemorial wisdom goes on to speak of the synthesis of all the universal forces and of its evolutionary course through the channels of personality. The blue starry canopy displays the primordial emanations externally manifesting the celestial planets and the stellar constellations of the zodiac. Most people mistakenly seek these primordial forces as located somewhere in the heavens above us, or erroneously believe that they originate within the boundaries of personality. Descending from the canopy, the four posts portray the differentiation of the Primary Being into the four elements of creation. Mathematically formulated in the microworld, the proportional arrangements of these elements give birth to all appearances perceptible to human consciousness. Science classifies these elements in their outer form as radiant energy or light, gasses, liquids, and solids.

The golden eight-pointed star the Charioteer wears on his head decrees the inner being's sovereignty over the solar light. Circling the area of the brain, the green wreath binding his golden hair calls our attention to the human specialization of this solar energy into mental forms. Eventually these patterns of thought will crystallize, and some sort of corresponding physical expression will materialize. Reminiscent of the waxing and waning of the Moon, the quarter moon faces on his shoulders reflect the fluctuating characteristics of our emotions. Like a swinging pendulum, they sway back and forth perpetually expressing themselves in various shades of severity and compassion. The breastplate or cuirass is made of brass, and protects the vital organs of the Charioteer: brass is the metal of the planet Venus, The Empress, who cautiously suggests the constructive formulation of our mental images, to protect us and keep us safe from undesirable ends.

The magical talismans engraved on his black skirt exhibit the unconscious forces as being of geometrical structure. They substantiate the concept that the subconscious medium of communication is basically pictorial in design. Each tarot card, in itself, is a magical talisman. These geometrical symbols expressing universal ideas have the most powerful effect upon human consciousness when we meditate and absorb their meanings. The black and white sphinxes in the foreground are a compound of the five senses. Many a writer has rightly called them "the propounders of riddles." We acquire all our impressions of the world of sensation through the combinations and modifications these five senses produce. The Charioteer is another variation of our inner self. He silently directs the vehicle of our personality, through the invisible reins of the mind, drawn by the powerful senses of knowledge and emotion. The wheels of the chariot demonstrate an important principle corresponding to Key X, The Wheel of Fortune.

Closely associated with the ideas The Chariot conveys, this principle speaks of the cyclic manner in which the human will unfolds.

Will-receptivity and speech complete this sequence of the dominant laws of our mental process. It follows discrimination because the conclusions we have finally selected, regardless of their nature or quality, truth or falsehood, have now been established, and now prevail within our subconscious. Therefore, the habitual word patterns we speak to ourselves and to others, the physical activity we initiate, the intellectual and emotional discipline we regard as being our personal will, are predominantly derived from the subconscious treasure house of images we created.

Exercise: Meditate on this card to expand your will power, by becoming more receptive to the inner self.

KEY VIII
STRENGTH

The key words the number eight suggests are rhythm, periodicity, fluctuation, involution and evolution, renewal, counsel, and convenience. Prominently displayed, the red lion astrologically corresponds to the zodiac sign of Leo. The Sun is the ruling planet of Leo, and the planet Neptune is exalted therein; therefore in this card, the powers of Key XIX, The Sun, representing the pair of opposites, fertility and sterility, and Key XII, The Hanged Man, reversal, are the most active. The major mental functions assigned to Strength are digestion and the sense of taste.

The woman attired in the white robe of purity is another aspect of The Empress in her most pristine state. The horizontal eight above her head indicates that she has incorporated some of the qualities of The Magician. The wreath she wears on her head bears flowers which are the developing seed ideas rising from the unconscious mind to materialize as the multiple images of our thoughts.

The red lion is a personification of the wild, uninhibited, primitive forces of nature, manifesting as the psychic and reproductive energy present within the subconscious. It is this reproductive energy that lies behind all our emotional and sexual expressions. It is this psychic energy that unfolds as the unconscious instincts that operate and drive the physical organism. These instincts are patterns inherited from past evolutionary development. The woman, as creative imagination, opens and closes the jaws of the lion, and makes it speak, indicating that she has the power to define and shape this reproductive force into any and every conceivable form. Therefore she tames and makes an ally of the mighty King of Beasts, who is another symbolic variation of the destructive powers of the serpent.

This woman's actions are a classic example that we must subdue and redirect our emotions and passions before we can gain adequate control over our personal actions and our environmental conditions. She leads and humanizes the lion by a garland of red roses, similar to those roses appearing in the garden of The Magician. This chain of roses represents combined and cultivated desires, selected and arranged on the self-conscious level. Combined denotes that these desires are restricted solely to those ideas directly corresponding to the principal objective. Cultivated signifies that these desires are a composite of the most constructive and creative images available to human consciousness. The chain of roses twists around the woman's waist and the lion's neck, forming another figure eight, identical to the one shown above her head. This universal signature of integration and renewal declares that the regeneration of personality has been effectively initiated.

Collectively this card is a pictorial description of the most potent and positive method applicable in the art of suggestion. Whether we are aware of its operation or not, our entire life experience is the manifestation of a continuous series of suggestions. From the day we were born, we have been consciously and unconsciously conditioned by our parents, our friends, our schools, the books we read, and all other types of media of communication we have been exposed to. Key VIII, Strength, speaks of the potential conscious control of our destiny, through the right understanding and utilization of the principle of suggestion. However, the application of suggestion alone in itself, will not assure you of beneficial or successful ends. You must be aware by now that the relationship between the conscious and the unconscious is much more complex than merely the selection of and concentration on an image. The supplemental element required is the ample comprehension of the mental and analytical process we have been defining in these lessons. When we follow this mental sequence in its proper order and manner, then the suggestions we invoke will bring us due rewards.

Additionally, the experienced recommend that the subconscious should never be coerced or forced in any way. To do so will arouse her fury and bring forth undesirable reactions, mentally and physically. Spoken words have little effect on her contents, rather as we have discussed previously, pictorial images are the language of the unconscious. In conclusion, we should look upon the subconscious as our greatest love affair, longing to know her well, and handling her patiently with gentle care. What we have reviewed about her nature in past cards should supply us with sufficient knowledge of her character and functions. By understanding her world, we can then successfully deal with her activities, and win her amiable companionship.

Exercise: Meditation on this card will expand your ability to apply the power of suggestion in its most positive manner.

THE HERMIT.

KEY IX
THE HERMIT

The key words the number nine suggests are: conclusion, end, goal, completion, attainment, cessation, perfection, boundary, and horizon. The six points of the star enclosed in the lantern numerically insinuates the astrological sign of Virgo, the sixth sign of the zodiac. Mercury is the ruling planet of Virgo, and Mercury is also exalted therein; therefore the powers of The Magician—concentration, and self-conscious awareness—are at their highest expression here. The major mental functions assigned to The Hermit are coition, or the union of opposites, and the sense of touch.

The Hermit abides on a mountain peak similar to those mountains exhibited in Key 0, The Fool. His white beard reveals that he is a personification of the Ancient of Days, a biblical connotation of our spiritual self, as written in the Book of Daniel. Regardless of his apparently advanced age, he is as ageless as the eternal youth and will forever continue to exist when all other things cease to be. Combined in their interpretation, The Hermit and The Fool seem to be of opposite nature; however, intrinsically, both are complementary to each other. Previously reviewed, the youth of Key 0, The Fool, is restlessly seeking adventure, and envisions future worlds to conquer. Here, the Old One is calm and collected. Having arrived at his selected destination, he carefully surveys all that lies below him, contemplating upon that which he has accomplished. The Fool illustrates the young and the young in mind, searching for new concepts to initiate, and rejecting those ideas which they believe to be worn out. The Hermit depicts the aged and those prudent in thought, leaning on the past, and retaining those achievements they look upon as proven and reliable. Not all concepts have merit or are constructive, nor do all past performances prove to be factual. Yet creative ideas do renovate and bring benefits to all. However, prospective action requires the prior examination and analysis of related practice established in the past. Therefore, human progress depends upon the union and balance of these opposites. This conjugal function is symbolically displayed as the hexagram star in the lantern.

The Ancient One holds his wand of initiation in his left hand inactive, indicating he has no need of its use for the present moment. His wand is painted yellow designating that the extension of light and the expansion of consciousness has taken place. Due to his accurate discrimination, the secret forces, distinguished in the card of The Fool as the black wand, have been wisely unfolded. The white snow on the mountain peak reports that some aspect of the unconscious has been purged and purified, and is now fixed into a definitive form of expression. Fundamentally, The Hermit is a portrayal of the collective unconscious, the recorder and preserver of all manifestation, and the container of all potential possibilities available to man in any given age or time. The golden hexagram star represents the solar light of the spiritual Sun differentiated into the six universal forces we spoke about in a past lesson. That it is encased in the lantern denotes that these universal forces are concentrated, manifesting as pure unaltered desire. Desire is the inner motivation that entices us into some measure of activity. In what form these desires appear in our lives depends largely upon our present mental states. However, every experience that desire evokes, regardless of its nature, accelerates some portion of personal growth.

The Hermit elevates the magic lamp of light in his right hand to guide those of us below to the perfection he has attained. The gray robe he wears signifies that the powers of human adaptation make it possible for him to combine, neutralize, and resolve all opposites in nature, therefore dissolving the seeming obstacles they presented. With love, he watches over us as we tread the various paths upward. With compassion, he shares all our pains, our struggles and disappointments. Yet his inner voice speaks to the strong and the weak, urging us onward, till we all scale the peak.

Exercise: Meditate on this card to increase your confidence and ability to achieve your objective.

WHEEL ᴏ͗ FORTUNE.

KEY X
THE WHEEL OF
FORTUNE

The key words the number ten suggests are: wholeness, law, embodiment, recurrence, distribution, reward, and conciliation. The planet Jupiter is the planetary force attributed to Key X.

Jupiter rules the sign of Sagittarius, Key XIV, Temperance, corules Pisces, Key XVIII, The Moon, and is exalted in Cancer, Key VII, The Chariot; therefore in these cards, this planetary force is actively engaged. In astrology, Jupiter is called the planet of good fortune, and is connected with all works of expansion and extension. The major mental functions assigned to The Wheel of Fortune are the principle of rotation or cyclicity, and the pair of opposites, wealth and poverty.

In its entirety, this card fundamentally displays the totality of being endlessly creating. Exhibited in the middle of the card is a threefold orange circle revolving around a common center. Combined, these three circles represent the universal and personal cycles operating simultaneously on all planes of consciousness. All our knowledge is derived by our careful surveillance of these cycles as they consistently recur in the world of phenomena. Assimilating this knowledge, eventually our creative abilities introduce and combine new elements—modifications which extend and expand these basic laws into a spiral of new expression and development. Therefore we complete what is imperfectly accomplished by nature. Which opposite unfolds—wealth or poverty—depends on our ability to grasp and comprehend these laws and principles in their true light. When we see things as they really are, then all obstacles disappear and nature becomes our collaborator.

The central point within the circle on this card relates to our most inner self described as reigning on the spiritual plane. The circle flowing forth from this center is divided into eight sections and corresponds to the mental world of creation. Eight is the number of the Sun, indicating that the regeneration of personality begins by renewing the mind. Continuing on to the next circle, the formative world of action, we find displayed the four alchemical symbols of Mercury, Sulphur, Salt, and the Universal Solvent of Dissolution. Mercury, Sulphur, and Salt represent the threefold nature of consciousness. These three essential qualities, when proportionately combined, create the Universal Solvent, the human compound that formulates, dissolves, and reconstructs all forms prior to their appearance on the physical plane. The outer circle containing the Latin and Hebrew letters, speaks of the world of sensation and matter. Here we perceive the end product, the result of all that has been in operation on the planes above.

The yellow serpent on the left side directs attention to those principles we discussed in Key I, The Magician, and Key VIII, Strength. This serpent illustrates the vibratory light of the Spiritual Sun descending into a more gross form. The ascending red Hermanubis is an Egyptian mythological god who, in *The Egyptian Book of the Dead*, acts as the guide of the soul in its journey through the underworld. This jackal-headed god denotes that the reproductive force residing in the unconscious is the impetus that evolves the lower forms of creation into the higher levels of expression and consciousness. In cyclic sequence, the serpent and the Hermanubis pictorially portray the descent of the primordial principles into the substratum of the unconscious, and the subsequent unfoldment of these principles as they rise to our conscious awareness. Therefore the circular motion of this wheel of life accurately depicts the perpetual merging of the conscious and the unconscious, and their reciprocating efforts to stabilize the personality. The blue sphinx is a synthesis of the four elements pictured at the four corners of the card. Its male face and female body demonstrate the conciliation of opposites, and speak of the liberation of humanity by its identification with the true self. The weapon the sphinx ominously exhibits suggests that this victory of liberation is due to the exercise of right mental discrimination.

Psychological observation of this principle of rotation reveals that many human beings unconsciously remain bound and chained to the same erroneous cyclic patterns throughout their entire lives. Confined within their false world of delusion, they pretend to escape the undesirable by superficial change in their appearance and activity. However to their dismay they soon discover that their problems, in one variation or another, remain basically the same. For those perceptive souls who discern the need of transformation within as well as without, and act accordingly, this principle of rotation responds by spontaneously accelerating consciousness to the higher, exciting levels of awareness and experience.

Exercise: Meditate on this card to accelerate the synchronization of personal actions with the universal laws.

KEY XI
JUSTICE

The key words the number eleven suggests are: poise, limitation, calculation, adjustment, formula, accuracy, interplay, impartiality, and equity. The scale the woman holds in her left hand is the astrological emblem of the sign of Libra. Venus is the ruling planet of Libra, and the planet Saturn is exalted therein; therefore in this card, the powers of Key III, The Empress (imagination), and the pair of opposites, dominion and slavery, attributed to Key XXI, The World, are the most active. The major mental functions assigned to Justice are action, work, and equilibrium.

The violet curtain draped between the two gray pillars reminds the student that the mechanics of the universe and its cyclic manifestations are the disguise that conceal the radiant light energy of the Spiritual Sun that is displayed as the yellow background. This knowledge, well known by the wise in the ancient past, and recorded in the tarot centuries ago, was scientifically presented in modern times by Einstein in his then revolutionary but little understood formula $E = mc^2$, defining that mass is a form of energy.

The golden crown the woman wears denotes that, in the physical body, this solar energy has its highest concentration in the area of the brain. The three square castellations of the crown speak of the threefold nature of consciousness as being gradations of this solar light, yet each possesses its own characteristics and field of operation. Set in the front of the crown is a blue square jewel. This crystal created by nature brings to our attention that the basic geometrical patterns of all matter are discoverable in the mineral world. The blue stone is an announcement of the reproductive principle of memory. The square setting tells of the mental measurement and classification of some specific form of knowledge. Form and memory are inseparable laws. There cannot be any memory of knowledge to draw upon unless there is some form in which this knowledge has been recorded and preserved, nor can any form continue to perpetuate unless there remains recollection of its existence. The woman, who is a personification of The Empress, wears the red Martian robe of action, and the green Venusian cape of fertility. The red robe implies that all action begins with the calculation of available possibilities discerned in the lofty levels of the abstract. However, the green cape of fertility declares that abstract thought has no practical use unless its theoretical formulas are brought forth into distinctive patterns of mental expression or physical objectivity.

The priestly stole descending from the cape is a visual allusion to the dual aspects of all creation, and to the simultaneous manifestation of these opposites. The black Y's embroidered on the green stole are the insignia of a yoke. A yoke is a device of human design used to harness animals, and also is an artifact fitted to a person's shoulders to carry a load in two equal portions. Black is a color tone designating the unconscious forces, and the element of earth. Interpretation reveals that, fundamentally, the creative powers of imagery control, direct, adjust, and balance the unconscious forces and everything that mentally and physically evolves in our lives. The golden scale Justice holds in her left hand is a product composed of the solar light, and insinuates that we must correctly measure and weigh this substance in whatever form it may appear before we can successfully define its function and equilibrate its activity in nature. She holds a sharp, straight sword, point up in her right hand, suggesting that effective mental action requires the concentration of effort, supported by acute observation and careful analysis, separating and eliminating all that interferes with our course of personal development. The function of work, or karma (the oriental colloquial parallel) speaks of the unfolding seeds of our past thoughts and activities as being the source of our present personal circumstances and external conditions. This principle of karma is well expounded in the biblical admonition "for whatsoever a man soweth, that shall he also reap" (Galatians 6:7). Therefore Justice, in its final judgment always prevails. Although the principle of karma cannot be destroyed, we can divert undesirable karma into more constructive channels by subsequently introducing positive elements. Collectively, this card is a glyph of the pursuit to bring equilibrium into our life and into all of our manifestations. To quote Eliphas Levi, from his illuminating book, *Transcendental Magic:*

> Equilibrium is the consequence of two forces. If two forces are absolutely and invariably equal, the equilibrium will be immobility and therefore the negation of life. Movement is the result of an alternate preponderance. The impulsion given to one side of the balance necessarily determines the motion of the other. Thus contraries act on one another throughout all Nature. . . . To operate always on the same side and in the same manner is to overweight one basin of the balance and complete destruction of equilibrium is a rapid result. Continual caressings beget satiety, disgust and antipathy, just as constant coldness and severity in the long run alienate and discourage affection. . . . works of wrath or severity must be tempered by those of beneficence and love.*

Exercise: Meditate on this card to establish a greater degree of equilibrium.

---

*Eliphas Levi, *Transcendental Magic* (York Beach, ME: Samuel Weiser, 1968; London: Rider & Co., 1968; first published in 1898), pp. 213, 216.

THE HANGED MAN.

KEY XII
THE HANGED MAN

The key words the number twelve suggests are: completeness, reflection, inversion, impressionability, focus, permanence, elimination, liberation, and surrender. The planet Neptune is the planetary force attributed to Key XII. Neptune is the coruler of Pisces (Key XVIII), The Moon, and is exalted in the sign of Leo (Key VIII), Strength; therefore in these cards, this planetary force is actively engaged. The Roman god, King Neptune, reigns over all the seas, and mythologically corresponds to The Hanged Man who is esoterically described as The Spirit of the Mighty Waters. In astrology, Neptune, the planet of inversion, is associated with psychic and mystical experiences, and with the practical unfoldment of these supersensory powers. The major mental functions assigned to The Hanged Man are reversal, and suspended mind.

For those of you inclined to pursue the deeper transcendental knowledge concealed in the tarot, pictured here are the seed ideas which can be an aid to interpret and to extend the comprehension of what is obscurely referred to in mystical terminology as the waters of life in the Bible, the first matter in alchemy, the mother deep of oriental philosophy, the underworld in mythology, and the magic circle and the triangle of art in ceremonial magic. Metaphysically, they speak of the universal substance from which all things are made.

Illustrated, we see a man hanging upside down, his right leg tied to a tree resembling a Tau Cross, bearing green foliage.

His left leg is bent behind his right leg, duplicating another cross. His hands are folded behind his back, and the bend of his arms forms the base of an inverted triangle of which the point of his hair is the apex. The Tau Cross is an insignia of Key XXI, The World, representing the pair of opposites, dominion and slavery, and astrologically, Saturn, the planet of limitation. This tree bearing green foliage insinuates that all productivity and evolving dominance over the forces of nature are due to the ability to limit and adapt this universal substance into whatever forms desired. The Hanged Man's red tights, parallel in color to the red robe of The Magician, indicates that some intention has been consciously formulated. The blue coat he wears coincides with the unconscious waters of The High Priestess. Upon her pliable substance, The Magician has imprinted his selected premise by an act of concentration. This consummation is visually displayed as the red belt that binds the blue coat. Imitating an equal arm cross, the legs of The Hanged Man demonstrate that The Emperor has taken an accurate measurement, and has arranged and classified the four elements in their proper order. The triangle, a symbol of the generating activity of The Empress, declares that this entire psychological process is in active elaboration within the womb of the unconscious.

In "The Thirty-Two Paths of Wisdom," The Hanged Man is called "The Stable Intelligence."* Its commentary informs us that within the substratum of the unconscious is recorded and permanently preserved the total history of the evolutionary development of the universe, and all the forces manifested therein. This history includes our entire collective knowledge and experience. Therefore the evolutionary past of the universe, and of humanity, can be recovered when we seek its restoration in a prescribed manner. Careful meditation on this card will reveal that this in-

---

*"The Thirty-Two Paths of Wisdom" in *Sepher Yetzirah: The Book of Formation*, translated from Hebrew by W. Wynn Westcott (London: Watkins, 1911). A revised edition was printed in 1980 by Samuel Weiser, New York. For another translation of "The Thirty-Two Paths of Wisdom" see Appendix 2 of *Sefer Yetzirah: The Book of Creation in Theory and Practice*, translated by Aryeh Kaplan (York Beach, ME: Samuel Wesier, 1990).

verted man has arrived at a degree of intense concentration and mental introspection, and is withdrawn from all contact with outer appearances and activities. Here the mental sequence has been rightly implemented. Its exercise has made it possible for him to consciously descend to the greatest depths of the unconscious. On the surface he seems to be in a tranquil state; however, the golden halo surrounding his head implies that within himself he is actively engaged, undergoing an illuminating experience. This enlightenment he receives is a communication of a distinct phase or aspect of the Universal Law. One of the most sublime of masters, who lived in this illuminating state of consciousness consistently throughout his life, spoke of it as "I and my Father are one (John 10:30)."

In Key XI, Justice, equilibrium revealed that adjustments of personality were required. Now, revelation of some universal principle awakens our awareness that certain personal thoughts and actions are the obstacles which lie behind our problems and hinder the achievement of our goals. This induces the necessity of their reversal. In its most spiritual exposition The Hanged Man is a glyph of true surrender; the complete suspension of personality, and the merging of the human ego with the one identity, our inner self.

Exercise: Meditate on this card to influence the reversal of undesirable habitual patterns of thought and action.

KEY XIII
DEATH

The number thirteen suggests the key words: love, unity, putrefaction, change, increase, purification, rebirth, destination, and perpetuity. The headgear of the knight resembles the beak of an eagle. The eagle, a symbol of human desire at its spiritual height, is one of the astrological emblems of the zodiac sign of Scorpio. The planets Mars and Pluto are co-rulers of Scorpio, and the planet Uranus is exalted therein; therefore in this card, the powers of Key XVI (The Tower), the opposites of grace and sin; Key XX (Judgement), decision; and Key 0 (The Fool), cultivation, are the most active. The major mental functions assigned to Death are motion and transformation. In the picture we see a skeleton in the armor of a knight riding a white horse. The skeleton is a personification of time, and time is a restrictive factor which eventually introduces physical death and the decomposition of all forms of matter. A skeleton is also the supporting frame of the physical body and the basis of all growth, suggesting the inception of life and its development. Symbolizing both beginnings and endings, Death implies the unification of all contrary forces by their reduction to a single essence.

The protective armor of iron, a metal corresponding to the fiery planet Mars, and the conspicuous red eye of the white horse, draw our attention to the principles associated with Key IV, The Emperor, inductive reasoning and the sense of sight, as having an operative role in this card's disintegrating actions. Psychologically, these activities demonstrate the continuing discriminative practice of analysis, which subsequently provokes the destruction of adverse mental patterns.

The knight mounts a violet saddle. Violet, a color corresponding to Jupiter, planetary ruler of Key X, The Wheel of Fortune, indicates that Death's inevitable victory over all forms of creation is a spiritual exercise to expand consciousness. The white horse the knight directs is in motion and designates perpetual transformation. No form present in nature, or conceived by human beings, can remain fixed forever, or be thought of as having arrived at its ultimate stage. Change is continuous, and this propels eternal progress. The horse has trampled over a king, doing away with the primitive ideas of divine and supreme rulership. The same awaits the prelate, the woman, and the child, destroying past conceptions of religion, and the status of women and children. The fish-headed mitre the prelate wears pertains to the passing away of the Piscean Age, and the coming of the Age of Aquarius.

"The King is dead," proclaims the knight, a declaration that many predominating beliefs we hold to be sacred have worn out their usefulness. They must now be dissolved and the energy confined be released, then we can further evolve the vehicle of personality by the reorganization of this energy into new interpretations. Inscribed upon the black banner Death holds in its left hand is a white five-petaled Tudor Rose. This rose represents the will, desire, and the five senses. Desire is an expression of will, and as we previously stated, all desires are based in one of the five senses. Therefore, the senses must be purged in order to eliminate the memory patterns of sensations we no longer wish to retain. The five points of the rose take the form of an inverted pentagram. The pentagram is a sign used in ceremonial magic by the magician to evoke and banish forces present in the unconscious. Here, the pentagram's single point down suggests that we are dealing with the unbalanced forces of nature. These forces are usually spoken of in books of magic as the demonic powers. Our conscious recognition of their existence is an essential requirement before we can initiate by an act of will, the banishment and resolution of these forces.

Present within this card lies the most sacred and recondite knowledge concerning the inner power upon which the universe is founded. The tarot reports that the animating force that extends our consciousness to the higher levels of perception is the same impetus which on the physical plane provides us with physical bodies. However this force misdirected and misapplied, as it usually is, unfortunately, leads to undesirable experiences, strife, and sorrow. Sigmund Freud, who enriched our knowledge regarding our behavior, basically limited his psychological studies and experiments to the sexual instinct of this inner power. Others who evolved from the Freudian school proceeded to elaborate upon other avenues of its expression. The tarot acknowledges and expands on their cognitions, and clearly states that unless the spiritual and mystical implication of these instinctive expressions is considered, understood, and rightly unfolded, humanity will continue to be haunted and beset by the problems they present.

In the background, the position of the ship denotes the direction the reproductive waters of life flow. Those who comprehend its mystical significance can follow the course of these waters to their source. Above the fall, behind the twin towers of personality, lies our objective, the Rising Sun of Rebirth. There, we share in the higher states of knowing. Those acquainted with the school of yoga will find here the secret key to awaken kundalini, the serpent-power.

Exercise: Meditate on this card to gain deeper insight into the meaning and motive behind our emotional and reproductive instincts.

TEMPERANCE.

KEY XIV
TEMPERANCE

The key words the number fourteen suggests are: purpose, art, assistance, support, combination, proportion, probation, reconciliation, and improvement. Astrologically, the iris flowers insinuate that the sign Sagittarius corresponds to this card. The planet Jupiter is the ruler of Sagittarius; therefore the principles associated with Key X, The Wheel of Fortune, rotation, and the pair of opposites, wealth and poverty, are the most active. The major mental functions assigned to Temperance are verification and wrath.

The golden disk on its forehead obviously identifies the central figure as the Archangel Michael, who "Like unto God," is the angel of the Sun, and of the element of fire. Yet, the yellow iris flowers draw our attention to the mythological Iris, messenger of the Olympian gods, particularly Zeus and Hera. She descends to earth on a rainbow and communicates their commands to the immortals. In the tarot's more subtle manner of correspondence, the arrow, emblem of Sagittarius, is associated with the virgin huntress Diana-Artemis, twin sister of the solar god Apollo, and the maiden representation of the triple-moon goddess. This white moon goddess was a continuation of the archaic pagan religion, an age when women were looked upon as being the dominant sex. Designated throughout the tarot, these anthropomorphic expressions of forces and principles active in both human beings and the universe, can be very revealing and rewarding when we study their allegorical activities as recorded in mythology.

As the androgynous universal male and female, the angel is a personification of our inner self in action, manifesting as the immortal soul or, psychologically defined, the human ego. The ego, the cognitive element operating in personality, constitutes feelings of individuality, and in our lives it plays the role of messenger and an administrator dispensing due rewards and punishments. Embroidered on the collar of the white robe of wisdom and purity are the Hebrew letters IHVH, Tetragrammaton, translated in the Old Testament as God. This divine name is the fundamental formula upon which the collective knowledge the tarot evokes is based and classified. Its interpretation is too complex to discuss in this preliminary study, however, personal meditation on the tarot cards, and the elaboration of the suggestions they unfold, will increase your understanding of its meaning. No knowledge, regardless of its esoteric nature, can remain hidden from those who are in persistent pursuit. Below the Hebrew letters is a golden triangle enclosed within a white square. This geometrical inscription declares that the ultimate objective of the angel's vigorous operation is to restore the inner self's creative impulses into measurable forms, free from the colorations of error injected by human personality.

Composed of the radiant light energy, the two golden cups the angel holds depict the receptive characteristics of the conscious and unconscious mind. Eventually, the cups will reverse their positions and the unending cycle of action and reaction will complete one rotation. Drawn from the undifferentiated substance in the pool below, the triple stream of water pouring from one cup to the other illustrates the three essential components of consciousness—spirit, soul, and body. Their combination and structural variations formulate all the elements defining human existence. Temperance speaks of the modification and adjustment of these various elements into more adequate channels of expression. Theory is an important phase of any training; however, laws and principles must be demonstrated and confirmed. This verification is the result of continuous test and trial. Only by these active experiments can we subsequently introduce effective change in the personal make-up of our being. Therefore, the Holy

Guardian Angel operates upon the substance of our personality daily, mixing and blending its contents.

The right foot of the angel is immersed in the pool of the watery mind stuff. His left foot resting firm on the earth represents the concentration of the watery mind stuff into solid forms of matter. The physical gestures the angel employs reveal that the work he performs is a psycho-chemical process. Alterations in mental patterns effect corresponding changes in the chemistry of the physical organism. The following quote from *The Emerald Tablet*, ascribed to the mythical Hermes Trismegistus, eloquently describes this alchemical process:

> Thou shalt separate the earth from the fire, the subtle from the gross, gently with much sagacity; it ascends from earth to heaven, and again descends to earth: and receives the strength of the superiors and of the inferiors—so thou hast the glory of the whole world; therefore let all obscurity flee before thee. This is the strong fortitude of all fortitudes, overcoming every subtle and penetrating every solid thing. So the world was created. Hence were all wonderful adaptations of which this is the manner. Therefore am I called Thrice Great Hermes, having the Three Parts of the philosophy of the whole world. That which I have written is consummated concerning the operation of the Sun.*

Exercise: Meditate on this card to accelerate the transformation of personality.

---

*M. A. Atwood, *Hermetic Philosophy and Alchemy* (New York: Julian Press, 1960), p. 8.

THE DEVIL .

KEY XV
THE DEVIL

The key words suggested by the number fifteen are: inertia, restriction, opposition, stubbornness, obstruction, incongruity, adversary, and materialism. The devil's horns are those of a goat, the astrological emblem of the sign Capricorn. Saturn is the planetary ruler of Capricorn, and the planet Mars is exalted therein; therefore, the pair of opposites, dominion and slavery, attributed to Key XXI (The World), and the opposites of grace and sin, associated with Key XVI (The Tower), are the powers most active in this card. The major mental functions assigned to The Devil are bondage or limitation, and mirth.

As displayed, the central figure is a classic illustration of the Evil One, exhibited throughout the ages as the Egyptian Typhon, Baphomet of the Templars, the Goat of the Sabbath, the Serpent in the Garden of Eden, Satan of the Hebrews and Christians, among many others. This horned monster, a synthesis of deformities, certainly does not exist. Rather, it is a personification of our faulty perceptions, misunderstandings, and misdeeds, collectively accumulated in the course of human evolution. In the Bible, Satan was regarded as the deceiver and slanderer. Consistent with his past successful role of seduction, he displays the exoteric sign of duality with his right hand, which is to say, "all that is visible is all that exists, nothing else."

The inverted pentagram inscribed between his brow is a seal of black magic and mental inversion. This sign implies the denial of the unity of being, and is a rejection of the superiority of the inner self. The pentagram, with single point down, is the geometrical signature employed to evoke the demoniac powers, which are always present within the substratum of human consciousness. As long as we personally sustain the belief that our existence depends upon, and is subordinate to, the elements composing our physical environment, these unresolved instincts of nature will continue to exert a major influence upon all our thoughts and actions.

The Devil sits on a half-cube altar designating the incompleteness of outer appearances. His altar is the base of the chains that restrain the male, self-consciousness, and the female, sub-consciousness—the dual aspects of personality. The chains rest loosely around their necks suggesting that they may remove them at will. Their bondage is of their own creation, the result of erroneous conclusions based on the imperfect and incomplete knowledge of themselves and the universe. It was their ignorance that formulated this legion of confusion, which is a compound of the four elements in distorted proportions. The male and the female sport horns, hoofs, and tails, demonstrating that presently the lower and less evolved forces are actively engaged. Unless we chain and tame these wild, unstable, destructive elements of consciousness, we will eventually become their victim and their slave.

Everything God creates has its usefulness, therefore behind this ridiculous apparition must lie some hidden purpose of constructive and beneficial significance. The Devil, the master of illusion, is the limiting principle of the universe compressing the subtle radiant light energy into the grosser forms of sensation. This world of relative appearances is necessarily full of contrast and incongruities. However, appearances will only deceive if we accept them at face value. Our inquiring minds are always concerned with the unknown, so as these seeming inconsistencies enter into our field of experience they awaken our curiosity and lead us on to investigate their nature. With his arms the devil duplicates the gesture of Key I, The Magician, to convey that the principles he portrays are synonymous with the forces The Magician represents. The act of limitation suggests the collection at a center of units of power, which is the basic characteristic of The Magician's function of concentration. Careful examination will unfold that the same principle The Devil employs to create appearances of illusion, unveils and reveals their true essence when we apply its law in the manner The Magician wisely recommends.

In the text describing the thirty-two paths of wisdom, it is written, "The twenty-sixth path is called the Renovating Intelligence, because the Holy God renews by it all the changing things which are renewed by the creation of the world."* Reflecting these words of wisdom, the devil holds the flaming torch of revolution in his left hand, igniting the tail of the male, our self-consciousness. Paradoxically, his antagonistic formulas of restriction are the incentives that arouse and incite the analytical powers of consciousness to seek the origins of its bondage. Provocation of this liberating instinct inherent in all of us subsequently brings forth the creative innovations that accelerate the evolution of consciousness.

Exercise: Meditation on this card will confirm that all adversity, regardless of its undesirability, plays an important role in our daily growth.

Sepher Yetzirah: The Book of Formation with the Fifty Gates of Intelligence and the Thirty-two Paths of Wisdom, translated by Wm. Wynn Westcott (London: J.M. Watkins, 1911), p. 36.

THE TOWER.

KEY XVI
THE TOWER

The key words suggested by the number sixteen are: will, power, truth, unfoldment, action, purpose, usurpation, inspiration, death, and creation. Mars is the planetary force attributed to Key XVI. The planet Mars rules the sign Aries (Key IV) The Emperor, Scorpio (Key XIII) Death, and is exalted in Key XV, The Devil. Therefore, in these cards this planetary force is actively engaged. Astrologically, the planet Mars is connected with works of physical activity, the motive powers of the organism, transformation, disintegration, and generation. The major mental functions assigned to The Tower are the pair of opposites grace and sin, and awakening.

In the past, this card has been variously called The Tower of Babel, The Fire from Heaven, and The House of God. The gray tower, located and built on a lonely barren mountaintop, is a representation of the combined elements of personality. Like The Tower of Babel, this structure is an expression of confusion and ignorance, founded on the mistaken belief that outer appearances are the origin of life and activity, and its sole support. The falling golden crown is a characterization of the egotism of self-will manifesting within our consciousness the illusionary feeling of separateness from all other wills. It is the self-centered arrogance of perpetuating the individual superior will that is a major underlying cause of our cruelty of lesser and greater degree. A spiritual frailty in itself when misdirected, this self-will, self-preservation aggressiveness, is the power complex that erroneously drives human beings to take advantage of human weaknesses, suppressing and degrading others of lesser stamina, knowledge, and talents. It was this avenue of the instinctive impetus perceived in the human psyche that psychoanalyst Alfred Adler chose to explore. His studies and experiments with the destructive nature of the inferiority complex were a major contribution to the better understanding of human behavior.

Toppling the crown, the descending lightning flash signifies a selected course of action. Arriving at its destination, the lightning flash assembles into the form of an arrowhead, implying the concentration of power. Manifesting as the electrical substance of our thoughts, this fire from heaven is a projection and an extension of the Spiritual Sun within. No longer chained as in Key XV (The Devil), the male (self-consciousness), and the female (subconsciousness), are falling head first from the tower. Unlike Key VI (The Lovers), the male and female are fully clothed, disguising their true nature from each other and creating an inharmonious division in their relationship. Their reciprocal misinterpretation of experiences erected the false crown above, which sustains the continuing delusion of the exclusiveness of personal will.

The tower in flames, and the usurpation of the crown and of the two figures, is a necessary function periodically initiated by the inner being. With neverending patience and love, this inner being, who creates all things, is also the purging fire that initiates the destruction of the many inhibiting thoughts and actions we no longer need by initially awakening our awareness of their presence. When these awakenings occur, they temporarily have a shattering effect upon our mental and physical structures because they usually tend to deal with the reversal of patterns of ideas that we have held throughout our lives to be of unquestionable character. According to some Rosicrucian theory, this destructive influence renders established forms, and releases their energy to make way for new forms to emerge. This is revolution (as distinguished from transmutation or sublimation), energy attacking inertia, the impetuous ejection of those who would enclose themselves in the confines of ease and tradition.

The black background portrays the occult forces veiled in darkness. The gray clouds speak of the incessant attempt to balance these hidden entities by integrating the knowledge they embody into conscious perception. The unknown frightens most human beings, yet these hidden forces are the source of our strength and enlightenment, and when consciously incorporated, understood, and developed, bring forth the liberation and freedom we are constantly seeking.

The twelve drops of light at the left correspond to the twelve signs of the zodiac. Woven together, the energies they represent formulate our psychological and physical make-up. The ten drops of light at the right are a symbol of the ten concepts of creation. These ten concepts arranged in a particular order outline The Tree of Life, the glyph of a philosophical and mystical system of which the ideas the tarot cards evoke are a part. These ten points of light are the primordial seeds upon which all unfolding laws and principles are founded. Using the tarot cards in the manner we have suggested does not require study of this intricate system unless you desire to pursue the more mystical channels.

Exercise: Meditation on this card will accelerate the disintegration of the undesirable complex patterns deeply rooted in personality.

THE STAR.

KEY XVII
THE STAR

The key words the number seventeen suggests are: hope, insight, tranquillity, disclosure, pursuit, reduction, guidance, healing, and solution. The naked figure holding the two vases is distinguished as the emblem of the zodiac sign of Aquarius. The planets Saturn and Uranus are the co-rulers of Aquarius, and the planet Uranus is exalted therein; therefore, the principles of Key XXI, The World (the pair of opposites, dominion and slavery) and Key 0, The Fool (cultivation), are the most active in this card. The major mental functions assigned to The Star are meditation and revelation.

Aquarius is the age of the great transformation, and is the sign of humanity in spiritual exaltation. The vision of this wondrous age has been long foreseen and foretold by the sages of ancient days. In astrology, Aquarius is connected with works of invention and humanitarianism. Contributing to the benefit of society, there has been within this century an accelerated advancement in all fields of learning, especially in the technological sciences. This expansion of knowledge has brought about a corresponding revolutionary change in the thinking and attitudes of humanity. We who are living in this dawning of Aquarius are now participating in a most exciting era of revelation and evolutionary progress.

The naked woman in the picture is another phase of The High Priestess who, as the Egyptian Isis, lifts a corner of her veil to reveal an aspect of her powers, or The Empress, as the mythological Venus, born from the foam of the sea, unfolding the mysteries of the universe. She kneels with her left leg on the earth, and places her right foot on the pool of water, indicating that the harmonious balance of the physical and mental worlds is established through the unconscious. The two vases she holds contain the total elements of personality. With the vase in her right hand, she pours our unconscious contents into the pool to signify that their substance is of similar nature. The vase in her left hand embodies the accumulated perceptions of our self-consciousness. The contents of this vase fall onto the Earth, whereby it separates into five lesser streams that indirectly flow back into the pool. All our perceptions of the world of sensation are based upon impressions we receive through the channels of the five senses, yet their substance in essence is also derived from—and consequently returns to—the pool. As the actions of this woman designate, from this pool the two modes of personality draw all their knowledge, and seeds of innovations to be evolved. In turn, all experiences, as they unfold, are simultaneously incorporated and collectively preserved in this universal unconscious treasurehouse of images.

The most important lesson we can derive from this card is the correct procedure and application in the art of meditation. True meditation is an active pursuit with a single objective in mind. To indiscriminately open the channels of the mind, as some erroneously do in meditating, is to surrender the human faculty of analysis to the uncontrollable impulses of the wandering unconscious. Subordination of self-conscious regulation is mental suicide, and its continuous practice can only lead to irrational thinking and fantasy. In the background, the yellow tree depicts the human brain and nervous system. The ibis perched on its branch is a bird sacred to the Egyptian god Thoth, who represents the principles The Magician demonstrates. This implies that meditation is initiated on the self-conscious level by an act of concentration, and its productivity depends upon retaining conscious control and direction.

The awakening that occurred in Key XVI, The Tower, has goaded the human instinct to seek the resolution of some active element within us which we suddenly realized is incomplete.

However, successful resolution of any inadequate element certainly requires some intellectual research and analysis to increase our powers of discrimination as we meditate upon a solution. Having equipped ourselves with reliable knowledge, we focus our consciousness by an act of attention on a selected point of inquiry, and hold it there. This single occupation of consciousness seals off our senses from outer distraction, redirecting them inwardly. The gradual descent into the depths of the mind stirs the unconscious into action, attracting all relevant images directly associated with our central thought. This progression is pictorially displayed by the water falling from the vase into the center of the pool, agitating its substance and causing concentric circles to form. As we mentally follow this unbroken flow of images, we eventually arrive at its very essence. Here, we observe the seed idea in its pristine state, free from distortions fabricated by the misinterpretations of personality. Elaboration of these illuminating perceptions induces adjustments in personality which, in effect, synchronize a portion of our consciousness with the universal principles.

The large eight-pointed star is the quintessence of being. The smaller stars are the differentiation of the quintessence into the seven interior planets (or the chakras of yoga). These planetary forces have corresponding centers in our physical body. During meditation these forces combine to initiate certain chemical and electrical changes in the organism. When these changes are permanently instituted, they bring about those supernormal powers we so often read and hear about.

Exercise: Meditation on this card will improve and increase our powers of meditation.

THE MOON.

KEY XVIII
THE MOON

The key words suggested by the number eighteen are: illusion, deception, reflection, dreaminess, moonshine, sorcery, intoxication, falsehood, and incorporation. By association of correspondences, the crayfish, an aquatic animal of the sea, is astrologically reminiscent of the sign of Pisces. The planets Jupiter and Neptune are co-rulers of Pisces, and the planet Venus is exalted therein; therefore in this card, the powers of Key X, The Wheel of Fortune (Rotation), Key XII, The Hanged Man (reversal), and Key III, The Empress (imagination), are the most active. The major mental functions assigned to The Moon are sleep and organization.

In Key XV, we discovered that our bondage was of our own making. In Key XVI, the lightning flash jolted us, usurping our egotism, and awakening our awareness of some erroneous idea we continue to perpetuate. In Key XVII, the tempest subsided, tranquillity took hold, and in meditation seed principles were revealed. Armed with these revelations, in Key XVIII, The Moon, reconstruction of our mental, emotional, and physical bodies begins. At this juncture reorganization of these vehicles is primarily a subconscious process.

As we prepare to traverse the yellow path of return, we observe at its very beginning, emerging from the waters of the unconscious onto the dry land, a violet crayfish representing consciousness in its early stages of development. Born of the watery mind stuff below, this crayfish resembles a scorpion, the zodiac sign of Key XIII, Death, suggesting that the reproductive instinct inherent within us, incessantly animates our journey onward to accelerate our consciousness to the higher levels of being. The narrow path of equilibrium earnestly declares that all our energies be singularly concentrated upon our objective. By employing this practice, we will increase our confidence and determination to succeed, and easily dispel all those distractions which defuse our powers, and reduce our impetus.

As in *The Dark Night of the Soul* by St. John of the Cross, during our journey we arrive at a point where we are suddenly confronted with the temptations of extremes.* At the right of the path howls a yellow wolf, a symbol of the wild impulses of nature. Straying from our objective, we irrationally seek happiness by uncontrollably gratifying our emotional and sexual appetites. As these impulses unfold to our consciousness, we stoop down to the darkly splendid world to taste their sensuous delights. However, knowing well that the longer we indulge, the more difficult it becomes to find our way back to sanity, the inner voice intervenes and sternly expounds that to resort to emotions unchecked is to submerge and bestialize love, degenerating life itself to the most primitive states of consciousness. As we retreat, reason prevails. But as yet, our concentrative powers are not at their peak, so again we go astray, distracted by the barking dog at the left, depicting the world of artificiality. Submitting to the rigidity of Victorian discipline, we find ourselves reflecting the cold uncompassionate concepts of a society instituting false laws to preserve the status quo, restraining the creative abilities of those who long to bring change and greater freedoms; human beings perverting each other as nothing more than mechanical vehicles, measuring human worth solely on material accomplishments and financial accumulations. Having survived—for the present—these tests and trials, we eventually find our way back to reality, and the growing realization that fulfillment lies in the balance of

---

*St. Juan de la Cruz, *The Dark Night of the Soul,* Gabriela Cunninghame Graham, trans. (London: John Watkins, 1922).

these extremes, therefore requiring their modification and adaptation.

We no sooner return to the path of moderation when we discover, to our disappointment, that it is not a straight upward climb. Rather, the path follows undulating ground, leading us to experience a succession of ascents and descents, revealing a certain psychological force at work. In the foreground, the green landscape commencing at the edge of the pool insinuates that, at first, great progress toward our goal is usually attained because we are using old habits and previously acquired knowledge, adapting them to new uses. However, after a time our achievements come to rest and further advancement necessitates the assimilation of new knowledge, and the formation of new habits. This requirement is designated by the barren blue ground that appears as we approach the fringes of the towers. We cannot always be climbing. When we reach a plateau of attested progress, we must stand steadfast. Those who do not understand the law represented here become discouraged and drop out. All things have their ebb and flow, flux and reflux, their pendulum-like swing between opposite poles. The Moon, with its waxing and waning phases, is an appropriate symbol of this universal law of rhythm.

In the background the two towers of personality act as a doorway to all that lies beyond. Their condition determines if we can proceed any further. Therefore the formulation of new rhythmic patterns on the subconscious level is desired. When these essential changes are established, then we will possess the adequate channels, mentally and physically, to take the next step forward. Beyond the two towers, a vast, unknown, uncharted world of knowledge and experience awaits. Those aspirants who have the imagination, courage, and strength to properly prepare themselves can enter and share in its wonders.

Exercise: Meditate on this card to induce the beneficial reorganization of the subconscious aspect of personality.

THE SUN

KEY XIX
THE SUN

The key words suggested by the number nineteen are: glory, truth, abundance, happiness, frankness, triumph, renewal, and illumination. The Sun is the planetary force attributed to Key XIX. The Sun rules the sign of Leo, Key VIII, Strength, and is exalted in the sign of Aries, Key IV, the Emperor. Therefore, in these cards, this planetary force is actively engaged. The major mental functions assigned to The Sun are regeneration, and the pair of opposites, fertility and sterility.

In astrology, the Sun is a symbol of our individuality. This focus of solar energy creates what psychology terms the ego. Based on the moment of birth, the angle of the Sun, in relationship to the positions of the other planets, form patterns that determine the structure of the more gross vehicles we refer to as our personality and physical body.

All saviors recorded in the history of all religions are traced to sun worship. Observing what was believed to be the motion of the sun, its daily rising and setting, its pathway through the heavens resulting in the phenomena of the seasons, those in antiquity rejoiced, and looked upon the sun as the god of life, whose radiant energy fructified the barren earth with agricultural abundance. Annually withdrawing its powers of fertility by descending into the darkness of the underworld, primitive people perceived its triumphant ascent from the tomb of winter as a sign of hope and redemption.

Pictured we see a naked child, mounted on a grayish-white mare, without saddle or bridle, carrying an orange banner in its left hand. The child is the son of the Spiritual Sun, manifested on Earth in human form. Having nothing to hide, its nakedness is the exposition of an advanced stage of consciousness, free from all disguise and delusion. In the Bible, a master of wisdom expounded, "Except ye be converted, and become as little children, ye shall not enter into the kingdom of heaven" (Matthew 18:3). The child, an expression of innocence, exemplifies this biblical verse, suggesting that the transformation of humanity depends upon the renewal of the mind. This renewal is the work of both the Sun and Moon, universal symbols of the two aspects of our personality. Their constitution must be constantly under our scrutiny and adjustments made accordingly.

The child wears a wreath of six roses, resembling the crown of a king. Upon contemplation the meaning unfolds: that the cultivation of our desires is mentally required to harmoniously combine the universal forces at play within us. The red feather of an eagle set in the child's yellow hair speaks of visionary and creative abilities, and the unrelenting human pursuit to realize its highest aspirations. The horse, a domesticated animal, depicts the forces of nature after they have been specialized by the selected power of the human will. As we traversed the path of moderation in Key XVIII (The Moon), new rhythmic patterns were subconsciously established. Here, these patterns are reflecting effectively throughout our character, so now, without great effort or need of a bridle to control its sense of direction, the horse is automatically leading us toward our objective.

The nipples and the navel of the child form the points of a water triangle, a motif of The Hanged Man. Like The Fool, The Magician, and The Hermit, the child carries a wand or measuring stick. These signs tend to imply that the mental and physical analysis of the secret forces involved has been successfully completed, and has taken effect; therefore the wand sports a waving banner to inform us that victory is assured at this stage. As an extension of the two towers of personality, the gray wall in the background acts as a barrier to the many who seek to enter into the higher states of consciousness the child enjoys. The wall represents the mistaken conception of appearances construed by the human imagination in response to sense perceptions. When we rely solely on our physical senses, they become an obstruction to our further progress. The world of form certainly exists, but external appearances are incomplete. Observation of the total picture is desired. Outer sensory reports must be balanced with the revelation of their inner essence. Only then can we arrive at a true judgment of the construction of thought and matter, and its significance in relation to our lives.

The four sunflowers behind the wall illustrate the four evolving stages of the solar energy. The three sunflowers at the left correspond to the mineral, vegetable, and animal kingdoms, and to the elements of earth, air, and water. The single sunflower at the right is a representation of natural human being and the element of fire. Each human being, the microcosm, the compendium of all the elements and forces in the universe, is the only creature in the scale of creation with the degree of consciousness to rise above the wall of the senses and enter into the Garden of Eden. A child shall lead them, therefore the four sunflowers face the child, indicating that they depend on him for their further development and evolutionary advancement. This child is the only gateway to light, liberty, life, and love, and its purpose is the complete emancipation of the human race.

Exercise: Meditate on this card to influence the regeneration of the mind.

KEY XX
JUDGEMENT

The key words suggested by the number twenty are: deliverance, awakening, salvation, prophecy, destiny, announcement, gateway, everlasting, and immortality. Pluto is the planetary force attributed to Key XX. The planet Pluto is the co-ruler of the sign of Scorpio, Key XIII (Death). Therefore, in this card, this planetary force is actively engaged. The major mental functions assigned to Judgement are decision and realization.

Astrologically, Pluto is connected with the subconscious workings of the body, the mental and physical transmuting actions which lead us to the higher states of consciousness, the conscience, our inner prompter that helps us judge right from wrong, and with beginnings and endings. In Greek mythology, as Hades, ruler of the underworld, Pluto is personified as a just and responsible magistrate, whose judgments may temporarily bring unhappiness and suffering, yet, his wise decisions consequently provoke the purging, purification, and growth of the human soul. Before we begin with our interpretation, we desire your attention and understanding. Though there is much we would like to convey, here we are dealing with exalted states of consciousness difficult to describe. In this card, as in Key XXI, The World, words become limitations and are inadequate. Only by personal experience of this fourth-dimensional world can you ever know and feel the ecstasy it unfolds.

Hovering above, holding a trumpet in his hands is the Archangel Gabriel, a Hebrew word meaning "the Strength of God." Gabriel, another aspect of our inner self, shows the flaming hair and wings of mixed colors, indicating that he is a compound of all the universal forces we have reviewed. The predominance of violet in the wings, a color-tone associated with Jupiter, the planet of expansion, predicates that the unification of the human being into a total being is at hand. The angel wears the blue robe of memory and reflection, which identifies him as the root and ruler of the element water. Therefore his activities are synonymous with the principles of The High Priestess. As you will recall, the stream of consciousness had its beginning with her appearance. Displayed below in Key XX, we perceive that this stream of life has arrived at its final destination. Its collection suggests the fusion of the watery substance into some sort of definitive form. Portraying evolution as reported in Genesis, the animating fire of the Self descends into the world of phenomena through the waters of creation.

The gray clouds which tend to conceal the angel correspond to the element of air and to the plane of formation, where the balance of consciousness continuously takes place. The mental patterns formulated here obstruct the direct observation of the inner spirit from those who erroneously base their thoughts and actions primarily upon outer sensations. As usually presented in the tarot, the male and the female in the foreground are symbols of the dual aspects of our consciousness. Their illuminating reciprocal activities have begotten the child. As regenerated personality, this child leads the way as we seek return to the Source of All. The human figures arise from their tombs of material bondage in response to the blast of the angel's trumpet, awakening all from the illusion of separate existence. The tombs, an expression of the physical plane as well as our physical body, float on the surface of the water mind-stuff, insinuating that its substance sustains all things created in the universe.

Reading from right to left, as in Hebrew script, the woman with her arms outstretched forms the letter L, the sign of the Mourning of Isis and of the sublimation of subconsciousness. As the only active figure directly below, she receives full force the magical influence pouring from the trumpet. The child in the center lifts both of his arms to reproduce the letter V, the sign of Apophis, the destroyer. He demonstrates the power of renewal and rebirth, which is the result of constructively directing the reproductive forces. The male at the left folds his arms on his chest forming the letter X, the sign of Osiris Risen. Representing self-consciousness, he remains comparatively inactive, fixed in meditation upon the Self above. The letters the trio collectively display, produce the Latin symbol of LVX, designating that their coordination initiates the extension of light. These mythological characters, Isis, Apophis, and Osiris, also reveal the ancient Greek formula, IAO, still effectively in use. This mysterious intonation stimulates certain psychological and chemical reactions when properly pronounced.

The measurement of the banner waving from the trumpet is a square of five units, totaling twenty-five, the number corresponding to the Magical Kamea of Mars. By special methods these planetary squares yield geometrical signatures used in the practice of talismanic magic. The planet Mars calls our attention to Key XVI, The Tower, where we experienced sudden awakenings of enlightenment, but of short duration. However the path of this card titled, "The Perpetuating Intelligence," speaks of an illuminating state of consciousness without interruption.

Judgement, sometimes called The Last Judgement, implies that at this point the weighing of evidence has been completed, and decisions have been made. Therefore there is no longer need for further evaluation of the facts, or debate, pro or con. Here, the resurrection of the soul sets the stage for our personal realization of immortality and the final liberation into the eternity of being.

Exercise: Meditate on this card to inspire this great awakening in your life.

THE WORLD.

KEY XXI
THE WORLD

The key words suggested by the number twenty-one are: inertia, perseverance, crystallization, synthesis, fusion, freedom, and equilibrium. Saturn is the planetary force attributed to Key XXI. The planet Saturn rules the sign of Capricorn, Key XV (The Devil), co-rules the sign of Aquarius, Key XVII (The Star), and is exalted in the sign of Libra, Key XI (Justice). Therefore in these cards, this planetary force is actively engaged. The major mental functions assigned to The World are the pair of opposites, dominion and slavery, and cosmic consciousness. Astrologically, the planet Saturn is connected with limitation, restriction, and the outward forms of things.

In the beginning, The Fool, abiding on a barren mountaintop, prepares to descend into the world of phenomena to pursue the realization of his inner vision. The journey has now come to an end, and his visions have been fulfilled. So in the center of the picture, this same androgynous figure stands unsupported in space, free from all limitations, and surrounded by the riches of its own creation. Proclaiming that the total integration of our being has been accomplished, the androgyne earnestly expounds the words of the master, "I am in the father and the father in me (John 14:11)." Wrapped around its body, the violet scarf depicts the cyclic principle of the mechanical sequence of events, which creates the outer world of appearances. This relative body of multiplicity of form is what conceals the inner existence of the Self, and confuses the minds of the ignorant, who seek intellectual definitions to THAT, without beginning, without end.

At this exalted stage of consciousness, the nakedness of Isis demonstrates that all obstacles previously ingrained in personality are dissolved, and the pure knowing of the inner self's essence is revealed. Her golden hair and breast, a symbol of fertility, suggest that the principle of creative imagination is at its peak, and through the channels of the awakened human, the endless potentialities of the eternal worker are incessantly projected into time and space, accelerating the world's evolutionary progress to the benefit of all people. Again the master's wise words illuminate, "And I, if I be lifted up from the earth will draw all men unto me (John 12:32)."

Her legs are crossed like The Hanged Man, imitating the number four, her arms form the sides of an upright triangle having her head as the apex, while drawing a line from her right to left hand would create its base. The triangle over the equal arm cross forms the alchemical symbol of sulphur, designating that human consciousness has arrived at its highest level of awareness and expression. Due to the consummation of the psychological and physiological changes we spoke of in past cards, the inner self's superiority over the four elements consciously perpetuates throughout the personality. The All-Father, All-Mother flare holds a wand in each hand representing centripetal and centrifugal motion. This spiral activity simultaneously winds and unwinds, integrates and disintegrates all forms existing in the universe. For your further analysis as you examine the card, take note of the other revealing geometrical diagrams the inner figure conceals. For example, the hexagram, the diamond, the swastika, and the number three.

The green elliptical wreath is composed of the reproductive forces of nature, woven into a definitive body, selected and finitized by the human will. The future development of these forces on the lower scale of evolution depends upon, and requires the introduction of the human element. The outline of the wreath resembles the glyph of superconsciousness. Its communication declares that the powers at work within personality, regardless of their characteristic quality, originate at this higher level of consciousness, and only when we fully realize that we are much more than our personality, will we be able to rise above the limitations we impose upon ourselves, and become the true masters of our lives. As in Key X, The Wheel of Fortune, at the four corners of the card, emerging from the gray clouds, are displayed the four mystical animals mentioned in Ezekiel and Revelation. However here they have no wings, signifying that in the world of formation, the transitory mind substance has been harmoniously equilibrated. Therefore, heaven is manifesting on Earth.

We repeat, there are no adequate words to describe cosmic consciousness, only direct experience will unfold its totality. Collecting my thoughts, some years ago I wrote a lyrical poem expressing personal experiences encountered as a student on the mystical path. In summation of the twenty-two cards of the Major Arcana, completing the operations of the Sun and Moon, I quote from its last verse.

> The twenty-first card,
> Brings our task to its goal.
> As the oracle speaks,
> Grand mysteries unfold,
> KNOW THYSELF,
> The angels ordain,
> The truth lies within,
> The spirit's domain.
> LET THE LIGHT BURN IN YOUR HEART.

PART II
DIVINATION

INTRODUCTION

Consulting the tarot as a tool of divination has firmly established through ages of successful performance its potency to adequately evoke from the depths of the unconscious our most inner thoughts, desires, and patterns of behavior. Perceiving that these human forces, proportionately combined, constitute the aura of personality and habitually dictate all human experience, we can readily accept the operative functions of the tarot as an accurately effective oracle revealing the past, present, and future. However, the tarot rejects fatalism, and wisely reports that the powers of consciousness can willfully adapt, adjust, and constructively modify any undesirable inclination that divination may unfold.

The following divinatory interpretations of the seventy-eight cards represent reliable basic guides, which in practice should include the diviner's personal intuitive elaborations and modifications.

DIVINATORY MEANINGS
OF THE LESSER ARCANA

THE SUIT OF WANDS (FIRE)

KING OF WANDS: a fair mature male, friendly, forceful, strong, and generous; in a position of authority; though hasty in temper, always just in his administration of power.

Reversed: prejudiced, inconsiderate, cruel, ill-natured, and egotistical.

QUEEN OF WANDS: a fair mature female, kind, generous, commanding and magnetic; firm determination in confrontation with opposition; psychic and spiritual yet practical.

Reversed: inimical to Querent; tyrannical and revengeful; an enemy to be concerned with.

KNIGHT OF WANDS: a fair young man, noble, refined, fierce, and impetuous; quick to action; may bring favorable communication regarding a new venture; possible change of residence.

Reversed: evil-minded, cruel, brutal, bigoted, destructive, and disruptive.

PAGE OF WANDS: a fair young girl or boy, highly intellectual, desirous of power; courageous in disposition; sudden in anger or love.

Reversed: domineering, superficial, unstable, emotionally theatrical; messenger of bad news.

TEN OF WANDS: charitable, generous, responsible; capable of carrying the load; persevering and not easily discouraged; shows reverence for religion and philosophy; always in search of new areas and ideas to explore; gain in travel.

Reversed: oppression, difficulties; impractically over-burdened with too many ideas and activities, rash; boisterous, uncompromising.

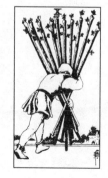

NINE OF WANDS: original, independent, mentally active; daring, fearless and adequately prepared to successfully defend his firm convictions, which are usually at variance with accepted opinions; health good or improvement following illness.

Reversed: danger or violence during travel; dispute with close relatives or neighbors; difficulties with religious persons due to skepticism toward their beliefs.

EIGHT OF WANDS: activity in undertaking; freedom and expansion in expression; swiftness toward selected objective; consistency in effort; visionary and confident.

Reversed: violence, warfare, theft or robbery; losses through gambling or speculation.

SEVEN OF WANDS: positive, militant, aggressive in manner, likely to arouse opposition, however very magnanimous, possessing a good sense of justice; fondness for strenuous activities; often too unrestrained in affairs of love; courage in face of obstacles.

Reversed: quarrelling, ignorance, insignificant victory; facing firm opposition; disappointment in love.

SIX OF WANDS: victory after strife; pleasure in work; happiness; deep and sincere in expression of love; compassionate, sociable, capable of holding positions of great responsibility; success in investments or any undertakings.

Reversed: wasted pleasure; insolence; loss of friends or the respect of business associates due to an overbearing pride in riches and success.

FIVE OF WANDS: bold, competitive, commanding, generous; irritates others when refusing to accept defeat; an undeviating pursuit of the fulfillment of desires; overwhelming others by enforcement of will.

Reversed: cruel, arrogant, violent, lusty, troubled by some illness; loss, dictatorial, prodigal; promiscuous activities.

FOUR OF WANDS: perfection largely due to personal labor; successful completion of enterprise; favor of powerful persons; respected, fortunate, ambitious, an advocate of innovation for improvements; gain through friends and travel.

Reversed: insincere, ineffective due to hasty actions or being unprepared; achievements in success or fortune of lesser degree.

THREE OF WANDS: pride, nobility, realization of hopes and effort; established strength; consistently in search of new adventures, ideas and friends; love of freedom and justice; exceptional ability of foresight.

Reversed: conceit, rude, insolence; liable to go to extremes through indignation, hasty words, or lack of judgment; disappointments.

TWO OF WANDS : dominion, boldness, pioneering, originality, active, combativeness; ability to resolve differences; frank, independent, dislike for all limitations or restrictions; possesses the insight to see things as they really are.

Reversed: revenge, shameless, overly ambitious, restless, unforgiving; quick temper, often acts too hastily on impulse.

ACE OF WANDS: force, vigor, strength, beginning, enterprise, innovation; concentration of will; selection of objective.

Reversed: absence of direction; uncreative; boring; weak-willed, easily influenced by others; temporary lack of progress.

THE SUIT OF CUPS (WATER)

KING OF CUPS: a moderately fair mature male, subtle, crafty, artistic, psychic; clothes himself in a veil of secrecy; externally displays a calm disposition, however internally conceals intense violent desires, though not particularly of offensive nature; friendly and disposed to accommodate the Querent.

Reversed: intensely evil and merciless; unrelenting thirst for power and wisdom to rule others and fulfill his desires; dishonesty.

QUEEN OF CUPS: a moderately fair mature female, good-natured and kind, yet not very responsive to others in need; vivid imagination endows her with the gift of vision; strongly attractive to men, and if married a perfect wife and mother.

Reversed: perverted, not trustworthy; an unstable desire for lovers to satisfy her emotional and physical impulses.

KNIGHT OF CUPS: a moderately fair young man, poetic, passive, very impressionable, tends to be mediumistic; eager to please; enthusiastic only when aroused by strong emotional or physical elements.

Reversed: lazy, indecisive, too emotional; withdrawn into a world of fantasy, therefore unreliable and unconstructive.

PAGE OF CUPS: a moderately fair young girl or boy, sweet, gentle, kind, very imaginative; indolent, yet when aroused is courageous; will be of beneficial service to the Querent; bearer of a message.

Reversed: selfish, overindulgent in pleasure; emotionally unstable, therefore unable to be of help to others.

TEN OF CUPS: permanent and lasting success; realization of one's desires; help and financial gain through friends or associates; very sensitive, yet emotional discipline brings forth a powerful influence over others.

Reversed: danger from overstimulation of emotions; tendency to overindulge in alcoholic beverages; addicted to drugs.

NINE OF CUPS: desires fulfilled; fondness for luxury and comfort; creative imagination, so not easily satisfied with limited ideas; suffers mentally and physically when misunderstood; may be self-denying at times to satisfy those they love.

Reversed: too much self-praise; can be easily led into foolish actions; conceited and vain due to his exceptional ability to gratify his every whim without much effort.

EIGHT OF CUPS: charitable, sympathetic, always ready to help the more unfortunate; love of travel especially by water; rejection of material things which he found were of little consequence; journey in search of a more meaningful existence.

Reversed: temporary success without further gain; emotionally unstable; journeying from one place to another without purpose or interest.

SEVEN OF CUPS: victory in sight, however there is no further advancement due to the indifference and indolent behavior of the person; often success gained but not followed up; fondness for pleasure, comfort, and a desire to satisfy the taste.

Reversed: illusionary success; lustful and ruthless toward the opposite sex; drunkenness; deception in love and friendship; difficulties with the opposite sex, and disharmony in marriage.

SIX OF CUPS: generosity, ardor, self-confidence, deep emotions, fruitfulness, enthusiasm, perseverance; financial gain through inheritance or business investments; the beginning of steady gain, increase, and pleasure; inventive abilities, fondness for chemistry and research, especially those things of mysterious nature; improvement in status.

Reversed: loss of legacy through treachery; danger of death on voyage through water; quarrel and litigation with business partner or relatives.

FIVE OF CUPS: usurpation and destruction of those false thoughts and pleasures which have hindered progress toward the fulfillment of the Querent's objectives; the capacity to accomplish much; gain through marriage; firm, determined, positive, though an unconscious disregard for the feelings of others.

Reversed: misdirected efforts; disappointment in love; sorrow; loss of a friend; anxieties and troubles from unexpected sources; severe illness.

FOUR OF CUPS: material success; discontent with the environment, desiring the inner world of mystical experiences; gain through mental abilities, inheritance, or marriage; fondness for home and mother, also loves to travel which may bring change in residence.

Reversed: highly impressionable and sensitive creating negative states and anxiety; gain through injustice; finding no pleasure from fulfillment of desires.

THREE OF CUPS: fondness of luxury and pleasure; enjoyment in merriment, dancing, eating, drinking, acquiring new clothes; an abundance of fortune and success; lucky in love; original, independent, rebellious against authority.

Reversed: physical and sensuous excess; too sensitive, easily offended; failing marriage; sexually unhappy.

TWO OF CUPS: love, reciprocity, harmony between opposite sexes; fortunate for marriage; emotional stability; strong devotion to home and family; friendly and very sociable.

Reversed: obstacles in love or marriage due to parents or financial difficulties; foolish and wasted actions; insecure and uncertain; changeable nature; Oedipus complex.

ACE OF CUPS: fertility, productivity, beauty, pleasure, happiness; fulfillment of desires; fortunate in love and marriage; successful in any venture.

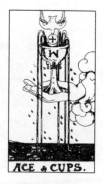

Reversed: difficulties in love; over-indulgence in pleasures; unstable desires; promiscuity; loss.

THE SUIT OF SWORDS (AIR)

KING OF SWORDS: a moderately dark mature male, very imaginative, firm in friendship; difficult to persuade; over-cautious and distrustful of new ideas, however will cooperate if you can win his confidence; a severe administrator of justice; has many artistic talents; tends to complete whatever he initiates.

Reversed: unreliable, harsh, malicious, plotting; involved in illegal activities; obsessed with self-glorification.

QUEEN OF SWORDS: a moderately dark mature female; confident, intensely perceptive; fond of luxuries; sexually attractive to men; a natural ability to get things done; demanding of others; yet at times very sympathetic and understanding.

Reversed: cruel, deceitful, unreliable; a dangerous adversary; emotionally perverted; ill-feelings toward the Querent.

KNIGHT OF SWORDS: a moderately dark young man, intellectual, skillful, knowledgeable, determined, analytical; an interesting and charismatic conversationalist; inclined to be domineering in love, but has deep regard for the feelings of others; will consider the thoughts of others only if based on learned opinion and experience.

Reversed: tyrannical and crafty; boring; emotionally childish when he can't get his way; immature in love; intellectually undeveloped yet attempts to impress others with a know-all attitude.

PAGE OF SWORDS: a moderately dark girl or boy; strong in conviction; acute in perception; frank in expression; mentally and physically active; liberal in thought and cherishes his or her freedom.

Reversed: frivolous and cunning; extravagant and wasteful; unwelcomed intruder and gossip; unexpected news of unforeseen nature.

TEN OF SWORDS: the end of obstacles or restriction; the dissolution of illusion; disruption of plans and projects; an eloquent and witty speaker who is inclined to be repetitious; strange and unusual happenings.

Reversed: desolation, ruin, defeat, unhappiness; an unfortunate occurrence; a serious misunderstanding with relatives or neighbors; unfavorable criticism.

NINE OF SWORDS: obedience, unselfishness, faithfulness, patience; profit from travel; temporary worry and despair, yet eventually a happy outcome; dual love affairs; success and gain through creative endeavor.

Reversed: cruelty, disappointment, misery; lying, dishonest; unfaithful in love; burdened with insurmountable problems.

EIGHT OF SWORDS: too much attention given to unimportant details; highly intelligent, acute, inquiring mind; generous, resourceful; argumentative and deceitful if emotions predominate; patient in intellectual study; determination regardless of restrictions.

Reversed: malicious, domineering, selfish without strong feelings of affection; views love in the abstract; lack of concentration; a blind sense of judgment and justice.

SEVEN OF SWORDS: limited success, due to a lack of consistency in effort; inclined to yield easily in face of firm opposition; unexpected turn of events; faithful and earnest in affairs of the heart; journey by land; secret alliances; some gains of money through friends.

Reversed: betrayal of confidence; unreliable and untrustworthy; troubles through women; good advice neglected; hopes and wishes unrealized; loss of fortune; employment with no prospect of advancement.

SIX OF SWORDS: success after warranted concern and difficulties; obstacles removed; pleasant journey by water; patience rewarded; fulfillment through labor; changes for the better; new opportunities earned; slow but persistent in effort.

Reversed: domineering, selfishness, conceited, due to overconfidence; wasted efforts; unfavorable change; cold and impersonal; danger in journey by water.

FIVE OF SWORDS: difficulties and inharmony; cruel, spiteful and injurious toward others and self due to a power complex, yet possesses mental and physical capabilities which can accomplish greatness if better understood and constructively directed; contest is over, victory or defeat according to disposition of Querent.

Reversed: defeat and loss; too radical in thought and action; troubles magnified; poverty in friends; disappointment in love.

FOUR OF SWORDS: poise and stability, freedom from anxiety following a period of difficulty; abundance after much struggle and confrontation; a platonic attraction to the opposite sex; peace and rest; contentment in mind and body; recovery from illness.

Reversed: disagreement with business associates; uncertainty in legal entanglement; losses due to misjudgments; troubles with the law; prejudiced and limited in thought.

THREE OF SWORDS: storm brewing due to past misunderstandings; however, honest and careful analysis will lead to solution; disruption of a mental state of inertia; generous and sincere in transactions of money; reliable in fulfillment of promises; deep sympathy for those in pain and misery.

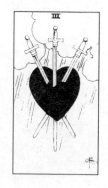

Reversed: quarrelling with relative or friend; too much love for pleasure; emotional difficulties due to loss in love or money; mental disturbance; heartless and cold in expression.

TWO OF SWORDS: fluctuation of character; successful negotiation of differences; indecision; a spirit of strength and determination following great suffering and pain; unselfish; a strong compassion for those in distress; a proponent of justice and law; delay in pursuit of goal.

Reversed: falsehood; selfish actions; self-gratification through excessive eating, drinking and pleasures; inability to complete any undertaking; emotional tensions due to uncertainty.

ACE OF SWORDS: fulfillment of activity; conquest of adverse forces; dispensation of power for good or evil; affirmation of truth and justice; the equilibrium of opposite forces or of emotional conflict.

Reversed: instability; failure due to negative thinking; lack of confidence; punishment resulting from undesirable activities; demonic possession in psychological terms.

SUIT OF PENTACLES (EARTH)

KING OF PENTACLES: a very dark mature male, practical, constructive; cautious and diplomatic in dealing with others; deliberate and persevering in labor; exceptional self-control; makes the most of opportunities; material increase.

Reversed: limited in scope; too materialistic; unproductive creativity; authoritative and emotionally cold.

QUEEN OF PENTACLES: a very dark mature female, kind, charming, good-hearted; reliable and enduring in any situation; careful about details; excellent capacity to measure the character of others; strong sexual powers of endurance.

Reversed: mentally lazy; superficial in thought; an inordinate desire for wealth or the possessions of others; foolish actions; promiscuous.

KNIGHT OF PENTACLES: a very dark young man, quick-minded and analytical in nature; witty and competitive, and very critical in judging conditions and people; industrious, serious, desirous of power and wealth; very patient and not easily discouraged in his pursuit of material gain.

Reversed: dull and heavy; jealous of the accomplishments and abilities of others; relentless in his goals to be superior, continuously pointing out the weaknesses of others to compensate and conceal his own shortcomings and lack of confidence.

PAGE OF PENTACLES: a very dark young girl or boy, courageous and benevolent; material accomplishments; firm in management; successful in practical application of knowledge assimilated; a message of good tidings.

Reversed: wasteful and recklessly extravagant; careless, suspicious, shallow in thought and knowledge; disorderly, prodigal; unfavorable news.

TEN OF PENTACLES: wealth, riches, material gain, pinnacle of success; fondness for pleasure and social life; hopes and wishes realized; a natural sense of discrimination; equilibrium of emotions achieved.

Reversed: clever in money transactions, but boring and dull; sudden losses of fortune; unhappy and emotionally insecure regardless of wealth; despair due to feelings of nothing beyond.

NINE OF PENTACLES: increase in material things; inheritance; fruition of labor carefully planned and developed; cautious and mistrustful of new acquaintances; a natural urge to accumulate great wealth and the comforts it can bring.

Reversed: easily discouraged; selfish, avaricious, envious of another's belongings; small in mind; failure to attain the goal.

EIGHT OF PENTACLES: careful and constructive, capable of expression in detail; skillful in material things; methodical in performance; admired for a demand for order; naturally intuitive, possessing strong powers of imagination.

Reversed: overly concerned with inconspicuous details; restrictive in thought; vain and boastful; hoarding and penny-pinching.

SEVEN OF PENTACLES: expectations unfulfilled; little gain after strenuous effort; gains of little significance; fondness for botany and horticulture; strong desire to achieve, even in face of defeat, therefore is considering new avenues of expression and labor which may be more profitable.

Reversed: unfortunate domestic experiences; desolation and sorrow; unproductive actions, creating despair; anxiety regarding financial speculation; loss of self-confidence.

SIX OF PENTACLES: prosperity; determined and practical in material matters; possessing great influence and power over the destiny of others; just, liberal, generous with all; highly respected for his good judgment; gain through intellectual pursuits.

Reversed: self-centered and insincere; material greed; unwilling to help the unfortunate and needy; exhibitionist of little talent; braggart; unfaithful in love or marriage.

FIVE OF PENTACLES: hardworking and knowledgeable in cultivating material works; usually correct in regard to form and custom; uncertainty creating anxiety and worry; possible recovery of some previous losses; tenacious in opinion.

Reversed: loss in business or profession; spiritual and material poverty; unyielding even in face of verification; an emotional and mental cripple; superficial; rejection by others.

FOUR OF PENTACLES: success, material increase, which is the result of responsible and intelligent management; an excellent ability to organize and place things in their right order; serious and contemplative; critical though in a constructive manner; may be unhappy even in his earthly prosperity.

Reversed: suspicious, prejudiced; a feeling of superiority creating a dictatorial characteristic; severe with those who disagree or oppose his opinion or philosophy; discontent regardless of success.

THREE OF PENTACLES: increase, growth, and realization of desires assured; constructive forces at work; money gained through speculation, investment or partnership; many friends of good standing and talents; fond of beauty and the fine arts; possesses creative abilities, though may not be aware of them.

Reversed: selfish, irresponsible, lack of conscience; difficulties with friends and acquaintances; conflict with superiors; narrow-minded and critical of the artistic abilities of others; lack of personal creativity.

TWO OF PENTACLES: harmony in midst of change; alteration of success and failure; gain through travel or change in occupation; fluctuating due to discontentment with self and conditions; a continuous drive to expand potentialities and to elevate position.

Reversed: wavering and inconsistent; unreliable due to a constant change of mood; easily influenced and led by others usually into foolish actions; emotionally cold and unresponsive.

ACE OF PENTACLES: great powers to achieve on the material plane; comfort and contentment; secure in money and earthly possessions; a masterly control over external conditions.

Reversed: a false sense of security and stability; deceptive and evil intentions; misrepresentation concerning matters of money or investment; material illusions.

DIVINATORY MEANINGS
OF THE GREATER ARCANA

THE FOOL: freedom; spiritual intoxication; inner vision; expansion in perception; lofty aspirations; love of adventure, seeking the unknown; the sudden and unexpected; a genius.

Reversed: foolish actions; carelessness; mania; eccentricity, stupidity; folly; mentally unstable; a false prophet; vanity.

THE MAGICIAN: skillful; wise; self-confident; intellectually quick; youthful in appearance; patient and deliberate; concentrated will.

Reversed: deception; nervous, irritable; hasty actions; lies; forgetfulness; lack of self-confidence; failure; indecisive.

THE HIGH PRIESTESS: hidden knowledge; fluctuating emotions; impressionable; excellent memory; psychic in nature; silent; interested in the Querent.

Reversed: acts too hastily on impulse; negatively receptive; overindulgence in pleasure; hostile to Querent.

THE EMPRESS: fruitfulness; happiness; success; imaginative and cultivating; sociable and affectionate; love for the arts; expecting new addition to family, or if Querent is a woman may possibly be pregnant or will soon be; compassion.

Reversed: anxiety in love, too emotionally dominated; barren; difficulties with friends; seeking material pleasures detrimental to inner development.

THE EMPEROR: orderly; stable; authority; ambitious, quick to act and accomplish; a natural leader and good organizer; conviction; pioneering; realization; passionate; aggressive.

Reversed: domineering; stubbornness; impatient; quarrelsome; quick loss of interest; impractical; disregard for others.

THE HIEROPHANT: divine teaching; intuition; determined; practical; favorable marriage; dutiful with family and friends; secrets revealed; manifestation; increase in money and possessions.

Reversed: greedy; insensitive to others; unyielding when angry; unforgiving; self-centered; weakness.

THE LOVERS: love, attraction; beauty; harmonious relationship with the opposite sex; resourceful; obstacles overcome; seeks change and diversity; cooperative; dual natured.

Reversed: indecision; foolish design; superficial in thought; frustration; discontent with others; failure in love or marriage.

THE CHARIOT: victory; triumph; sensitivity; tenacious; domesticity; devotion to loved ones; gain in property; patience required; vengeance for a past injury or offense; sentimental.

Reversed: defeat; quarrel; ill-health; emotionally immature; ruthless when in authority; promiscuous.

STRENGTH: courage; fortitude; action; magnanimity; honors bestowed; successful outcome; commanding; self-disciplined; endurance; regal; confidant; adventurous; idealistic.

Reversed: abuse of power; tyranny; emotionally arrogant; outspoken; dictatorial; explosive.

THE HERMIT: prudence; circumspection; illumination from above; conservative, discriminating and methodical in details; withdrawal from activity; discretion necessary.

Reversed: worry and anxiety due to unreasoned caution; concealment of important information; selfish ends; lack of self-confidence.

THE WHEEL OF FORTUNE: good fortune; success; exaltation; prominence; comprehension; travel abroad; positions of dignity, trust, or power in the kinds of business that are engaged in works of a philanthropic and benevolent nature.

Reversed: unsociable; overly occupied with success; losses through misjudgment; restlessness; uncertainty; ill health.

JUSTICE: legal proceedings; triumph for those in the right; just decision; conciliation of opposing forces; adjustments; peace and harmony; artistic; cooperative, and affectionate.

Reversed: corruption; complications or loss in legal affairs; excessive severity; reckless actions; vacillating and vain.

THE HANGED MAN: sacrifice; introspection; discernment; detachment from material things; conditions of mysterious hidden nature; spiritual perceptions; clairvoyant; reversal.

Reversed: suffering; clandestine; deception in perception; selfish; negatively passive; psychic disturbances; addiction to drugs.

DEATH: transformation, change; destruction, death as in the ending of past activity; secretive; mentally magnetic; possessing a desirous thirst to achieve power and reach high attainments.

Reversed: inaction; suspicion; cynicism; perversions; hopes destroyed; obsession for power creating a callous attitude and cruelty toward others.

TEMPERANCE: moderation; modification; mixture of due proportions and the reduction of excessiveness; good management; adaptation; outspoken; excellent foresight and usually right as to the outcome; long journey.

Reversed: undesirable and unfortunate combinations; discord creating separation; uncompromising; boisterous; too many irons in the fire.

THE DEVIL: material power and pursuits; firm determination; ambition; extraordinary efforts; emotionally cold in expression and demonstration; confrontation with limitations which must be dealt with; a selfish desire for money and earthly possessions.

Reversed: fear of change; obsession; violence; blind forces; evil actions; gives way easily to temptation; restricted due to ignorance.

THE TOWER: forceful disintegration of restrictions and limitations; usurpation of false images; courage; leadership; a constructive effort; strong competition; inspiration.

Reversed: quarrels; unseen calamity; sudden disruption of plans; distress; cruelty; emotionally explosive; danger of injury; deception.

THE STAR: high hopes; promising expectations; desires realized; inner visions; secrets unfolded; gains through friends or acquaintances; capable of dealing with facts; active in reforms; strong likes and dislikes.

Reversed: false desires; losses; fruitless dreaming; gullible; scattered effort; exploitation of others; insensitivity.

THE STAR.

THE MOON: fluctuation; idealism; secret matters; hidden enemies; psychic experience; benefits through help and charity, given and received; voluntary change in thought or actions; lurking dangers; fears and weaknesses to overcome.

Reversed: deception; false images; unstable and negative feelings; bewilderment; inconsistent in effort; inimical occult forces.

THE MOON.

THE SUN: happiness, glory, wealth, material gain; fortunate marriage; a harmonious relationship with the opposite sex; generous, honorable, responsible; successful outcome of Querent's aims.

Reversed: arrogance; extravagance; domineering; vain; losses of position, credit or esteem due to impulsiveness or conceit; egotistical; ill health.

THE SUN.

JUDGEMENT: decision; renewal; determination of a matter; the perception of right from wrong; change of position; beneficial financial prospects; detection of injustice; inheritance of a legacy; deliberate efforts; healing.

Reversed: low morality; lack of conscience; weakness; unjust decision; untrustworthy; illegal activities.

THE WORLD: synthesis; ultimate success; completion; reward; the crystallization of hopes and desires; control over conditions; serious and practical in nature; economical and prudent; executive in stature; a master in business and material things.

Reversed: restrictions; inaction; lack of progress due to stagnation; adverse forces at work; many disappointments and sorrows; stubborn and unyielding in face of the truth.

ADDITIONAL SYMBOLISM

The general signification of the four suits:

Wands: will, enterprise, beginnings.
Cups: imagination, desires, emotional activities.
Swords: action, conflict, forces of disintegration and inte-
gration.
Pentacles: material things and possessions.

The general physical characteristics of the sixteen court cards:

Kings: older men
Queens: older women
Knights: young men
Pages: young boys or girls
Wands: fair complexion, auburn hair, blue or green eyes.
Cups: moderately fair complexion, blond hair, blue eyes.
Swords: moderately dark complexion, brown hair, hazel
eyes.
Pentacles: dark complexion, black hair, dark eyes.

Further divinatory elucidations can be acquired by a careful review of those chapters dealing with the twenty-two cards of the
Greater Arcana, and the Ten Sephiroth of the Tree of Life.

DIVINATORY PRACTICE

CELTIC METHOD

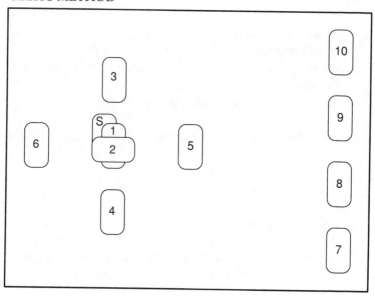

This method of divination is recommended as being most adequate in dealing with a single point of inquiry.

1. Select a card, called the Significator, to represent the person or matter in question. Limit your selection to one of the sixteen Court Cards— a card that most descriptively corresponds to the Querent. Place this card faceup on the table.

2. Allow the Querent to shuffle the rest of the deck to his or her satisfaction, while thinking earnestly of the matter under consideration.

3. Instruct the Querent to place the deck on the table, facedown and divide the deck into three piles toward the left with his or her left hand.

4. Now the Diviner proceeds to reassemble the deck from right to left with the left hand, keeping the cards facedown.

5. Turn up the FIRST CARD (top) of the deck; cover the Significator with it, and say: "This covers you." This card gives the influence which is affecting the person or matter of inquiry, generally the person's present state of mind.

6. Turn up the SECOND CARD and lay it across the first, saying: "This crosses you." This represents the obstacle that presently confronts the Querent. If it is a favorable card, the opposing forces will not be serious.

7. Turn up the THIRD CARD; place it above the Significator, and say: "This crowns you." This represents the Querent's objective and the best he or she can hope to achieve; however, these forces have not as yet manifested.

8. Turn up the FOURTH CARD; place it below the Significator and say: "This is beneath you." This unfolds the Querent's basic thoughts and feelings in regard to the matter, which have already passed into actuality.

9. Turn up the FIFTH CARD; place it on the side of the Significator from which it is looking, and say: "This is behind you." This reveals the influence which has recently passed or is now passing away. If the Significator is not facing either way, the Diviner will decide which side he or she will take it as facing.

10. Turn up the SIXTH CARD; place it on the side the Significator is facing, and say: "This is before you." This unveils the influence which is coming into action and will operate in the near future.

An example of the Celtic Cross Spread with cards laid out for a young male querent. His significator is the Knight of Cups and the first card is the Six of Cups.

11. The cards are now disposed in the form of a cross, the Significator, covered by the FIRST CARD, being in the center. The next four cards are turned up in succession, and placed one above the other in a line, on the right side of the cross.

12. The first of these cards, or the SEVENTH CARD, signifies the persons position or attitude in the circumstances.

13. The EIGHTH CARD signifies the Querent's house, the tendencies at play which have an effect on the matter; for example, position in life, the influence of friends, etc.

14. The NINTH CARD reveals his hopes and fears in the matter.

15. The TENTH CARD speaks of the final outcome of the matter, the result of the combined forces the other cards exert.

16. The operation is now completed. If the last card is of doubtful nature whereby no final decision can be drawn, repeat the entire operation, using in this case the TENTH CARD as the Significator.*

AN EXAMPLE OF THE CELTIC METHOD

The Querent was a young man with blond hair and blue eyes. The Knight of Cups was selected as the Significator. The matter of inquiry was not disclosed. The cards were laid out as mentioned above, and the following interpretation unfolded.

FIRST CARD: SIX OF CUPS (present state of mind): "Your question deals with improvement in a position or status." The Querent confirmed that he was concerned with a matter of promotion in employment, a position that was soon to be available.

------

*The Celtic Method is adapted from Arthur Waite's *The Pictorial Key to the Tarot* (York Beach, ME: Samuel Weiser, 1973).

SECOND CARD: SEVEN OF SWORDS (obstacles): "The opposing force—which can be self-defeating—and is a matter for correction, is your lack of consistency in effort. However, the card is well dignified, therefore the obstacle will not be serious."

THIRD CARD: THE STAR (the best he can hope for): "This card suggests that your desire for advancement can be achieved."

FOURTH CARD: THREE OF PENTACLES REVERSED (his basic thoughts and feelings, previously experienced): "This card speaks of a past conflict with your superiors."

FIFTH CARD: TWO OF SWORDS (influence recently past): "However, insinuated here is that these differences have been harmoniously resolved, therefore you will not be burdened with a situation we would consider as an insurmountable problem."

SIXTH CARD: KNIGHT OF PENTACLES REVERSED (coming into action): "You will soon be aware of serious competition from a fellow employee who is relentless in his efforts, and who will continuously attempt to undermine your pursuit by pointing out and exaggerating your weaknesses to others."

SEVENTH CARD: SIX OF WANDS (his position and attitude): "Due to many years of loyal services rendered, you feel most deserving, and more than adequately prepared to hold this position of greater responsibility."

EIGHTH CARD: QUEEN OF PENTACLES (influence of friends in the matter): "This card shows an older woman, married, whom you consider a good friend, and who is also an employee of the firm, holding a position of trust. It seems that there has been more than a friendly attraction and relationship here. Without question you can rely upon her aid, which will have much influence upon your superiors."

NINTH CARD: FIVE OF PENTACLES REVERSED (hopes and fears): "Presently your greatest fears are financial security and the anxiety of being rejected by others."

TENTH CARD: STRENGTH (final outcome): "Successful out-come. Your obstacle which is not serious can be easily corrected by formulating firm patterns of determination through increase of your powers of concentration. As for other competition fore-seen there is no need to worry. This card and the combination of the others, reveal that the elements are strongly in your favor, therefore you can be assured that you will acquire the position you desire."

THE TWENTY-ONE CARD SPREAD

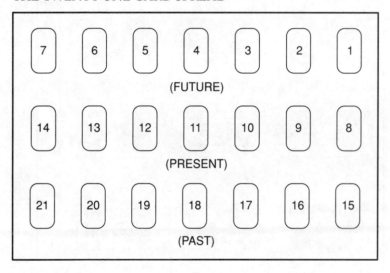

This method of divination offers greater freedom in interpre-tation, and is recommended for a general reading rather than a single question of inquiry. Human beings are quite complex and extensive, therefore no reading could possibly disclose them in their entirety. In our analysis we perceive and amplify predominating elements—positive and negative, conscious and unconscious—which emerge at the moment of divination, in a manner as to direct the attention of the Querent to their existence, and to possible solutions should they be of a nega-tive nature. More than one reading at a sitting may be imple-mented. With each spread new elements may unfold.

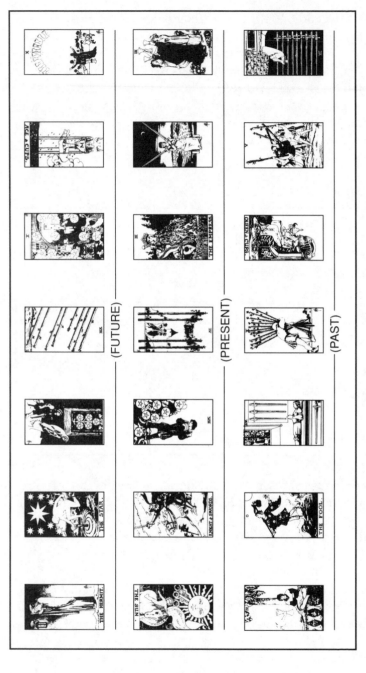

An example of the Twenty-one Card Spread with cards laid out for a female querent.

Memorization of the general meanings of the cards, combined with a fertile imagination, is suggested and required in any operation conducted. Practice makes perfect, and as you do so, accuracy in your interpretations will develop.

Allow the Querent to thoroughly shuffle the deck. Keeping the deck facedown, instruct the Querent to select at random twenty-one cards unseen. Place the remainder of the deck aside. Pick up the pile of the twenty-one cards selected, and proceed to deal horizontally, from right to left, bottom to top, three rows of seven cards, face upward. Divination begins with the bottom row which forms what is read as the past. The middle row of seven cards form what is read as the present, and lastly, the top row of seven cards form what is read as the future.

Read the cards in their order, right to left. However, if the continuity is not well-established, it is permissible to mentally rearrange the seven cards in any combined sequence which will adequately provide a reading of consistency and substance.

AN EXAMPLE OF THE TWENTY-ONE CARD SPREAD

The Querent was an attractive woman in her 30s, black hair, dark eyes, therefore the Queen of Pentacles was appropriate as the Significator.

The Querent shuffled the deck, selected at random and arranged into a separate pile twenty-one cards. The remaining deck was placed aside and the twenty-one cards were distributed into three rows of seven cards. The layout is shown on the opposite page.

Reading from right to left, the following interpretation emerged:

The PAST shows conflict, inharmony and disappointment in love and marriage; the result of an unfaithful husband and a covetous woman, who as you subsequently discovered was a close and supposedly trustworthy friend of the family. However, regardless of the distress this undesirable disclosure created, you were able to bear the load and endure the pressures courageously. The legal entanglements that followed eventually freed you from this period of difficulty and embarrassment, and the arrangements made left you financially comfortable.

The PRESENT reveals that you are quite content, independent, enjoying the better things in life. Your past history of suffering and pain has implanted within you a true sense of compassion for others in distress, and a strong determination to be of help. Therefore, those who know you well freely seek and value your advice.

You have been socializing quite frequently, and I see that your preference in relationships has been generally toward men younger than yourself. There is a gentleman you feel attracted to who has intellectual characteristics you highly admire, we may go as far and say that you're in love, and that images of marriage are again in full bloom. Though this gentleman is honest and sincere, presently he is financially insecure, therefore unprepared to take on this responsibility. Marriage at this time is not advised.

Your FUTURE unfolds a continuous prosperity, particularly in the realization of your desires. However, danger lies in overindulgence which can arise from little resistance confronted, creating an atmosphere of false perceptions and apathy. Therefore, it is suggested that these personal evolving powers of crystallization be well-disciplined and directed into the most constructive channels available. Avoid hasty decisions and actions, especially in speculative investments or business ventures, which will lead to losses not only of money, but the loss of very dear friends who have the tendency to follow your advice faithfully. The Hermit and The Star imply the development of a greater degree of insight and inner experiences that will bring an expansion of consciousness unparalleled in your present and past.

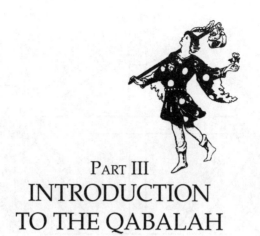

PART III
INTRODUCTION
TO THE QABALAH

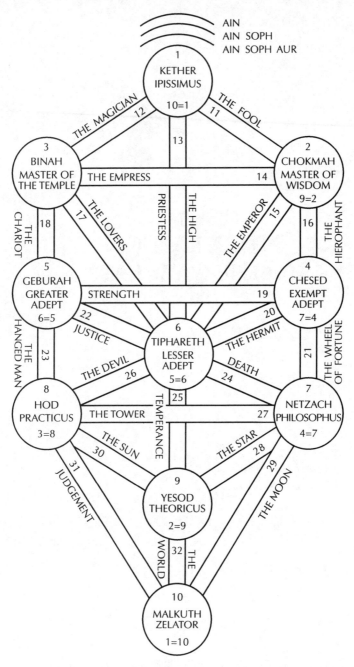

The Tree of Life. Adapted from the Order of the Golden Dawn.

THE QABALAH

Qabalah is an ancient theosophical system, a doctrine of study and practice that continues to influence all religious, mystical, and secret (or esoteric) schools of thought in the western world. Qabalah is a Hebrew word derived from the root QBL, meaning "to receive." This appellation refers to the custom of handing down esoteric knowledge by oral transmission. Its early followers contended that qabalah was first taught by God to a selected company of angels; after the Fall, the angels communicated this heavenly doctrine to Adam so the children of Earth might have the means of returning to their pristine nobility. From Adam it passed over to Noah, and then to Abraham who migrated to Egypt, allowing some of its knowledge to be revealed, whereby the Egyptian and eastern nations could introduce it into their philosophical systems. Moses, learned in this wisdom, laid down the principles of this secret doctrine in the four books of the Pentateuch, initiating the seventy elders into its secrets. Continuing in an unbroken line of tradition, no one dared to write it down until Schimeon Ben Jachai composed the celebrated work called The Zohar, a storehouse of its teachings.

Modern research investigating its dogma has discovered that its beliefs are similar to the yoga schools of the East, and that its principles are crudely reflected in archaic fragments of primeval practices uncovered in archaeological findings throughout the world. This has led the modern seeker and mystic to assume that this knowledge is available to anyone who may seek it, regardless of race, sex, culture, or location. Though the mystical doctrine and objectives of the East and West meet, our western practice differs somewhat from the yoga discipline as taught in the East. Evidence passed on from our ancient brethren confirms and supports the qabalistic methods, which were formulated especially for the western mind and body, and are the most effective for those of us born and living in this part of the world. The oriental formula certainly brings results to our eastern friends, yet its application can be detrimental to our progress mentally and physically, due to differences existing in the occidental and oriental evolutionary patterns of development.

Qabalah is classified under the following four headings: 1) the practical qabalah; 2) the literal qabalah; 3) the unwritten qabalah; 4) the dogmatic qabalah. The practical qabalah deals with talismanic and ceremonial magic, and has held the greatest appeal to the general public throughout the ages. However, very few grasp its true meaning and purpose, and even fewer can put it into practical use and get results. Many books written concerning this aspect of the magical experience too often confuse transcendence with sensationalism. Unfortunately, because most of these writers lack the laborious study and rigid training required, their misinterpretations have distorted its intent and objective, degrading its procedures and its operation into mere superstition and fantasy.

The literal qabalah is a cryptographic system divided into three forms of which Gematria is the most important. This coded method of word and number associations corresponds closely to the analytical processes used by modern psychology today, allowing deep-rooted subconscious thought patterns to be brought forth into the subject's conscious awareness. Gematria also forms the mystic's dictionary, his aid to correctly decipher and obtain hidden wisdom concealed behind certain Hebrew, Greek, or Latin words and phrases found in various qabalistic treatises, and within the Old and New Testaments; both works written by men well schooled in the qabalistic philosophy.

The unwritten qabalah is a mass of secret knowledge, never entrusted to writing, but communicated orally. Though this knowledge is not in itself of Hebrew origin, the qabalah has preserved its arcane teachings and practices intact to this day. The most inner mysteries of this esoteric instruction cannot be taught or communicated to others by words. However, its essence lies in the study of the dogmatic qabalah.

The Tree of Life, the diagrammatic compendium of the qabalistic system, is the magical pathway that unfolds these uncommunicable secrets of creation to its initiates (see page 108 for a depiction of "The Tree of Life"). Its geometrical arrangement and proportions declared that all creation is mathematically formulated, a truth sustained by scientific confirmation of the atomic structure of all matter. Composed of ten seed concepts, these evolving emanations of consciousness represent the intellectual and transcendental perception of what we term God, Man and the Universe.

THE TREE OF LIFE

The Tree of Life is a map of involution and evolution, a guide directing its students into the most creative and constructive channels, to expand personal consciousness to its lofty levels of reception. Numbered from One to Ten, the ten spheres of the Tree are called the Sephiroth, or Numerations. They constitute a system of classification whereby all thought, action, or forms of matter, past, present, and future, can be correctly categorized and accurately defined in essence and objective. Corresponding to the tarot's Major Arcana, the twenty-two connecting paths represent the subjective reactions these Ten Sephiroth evoke. In total, the Ten Sephiroth and the twenty-two connecting paths form the skeleton outline of the Tree of Life, whose Thirty-Two Paths of Wisdom embody the Entirety of Being. See page 108 for an illustration of the Tree of Life.

In the most ancient of qabalistic texts, *Sepher Yetzirah: The Book of Formation*, it is written:

> Ten is the number of the ineffable Sephiroth, ten and not nine, ten and not eleven. Understand this wisdom and be wise by the perception. Search out concerning it, restore the Word to its creator, and replace Him who formed it upon his throne. . . . The Ten ineffable Sephiroth have the appearance of the Lightning flash, their origin is unseen and no end is perceived. The Word is in them as they rush forth and as they return, they speak as from the whirlwind, and returning fall prostrate in the adoration before the Throne. The Ten ineffable Sephiroth, whose ending is even as their origin, are like as a flame arising from a burning coal.

For God is superlative in his Unity; there is none equal
unto Him: what number canst thou place before One.
Ten are the ineffable Sephiroth; seal up thy lips lest
thou speak of them, and guard thy heart as thou
considerest them; and if thy mind escape from thee
bring it back to thy control; even as it was said, "run-
ning and returning, (the living creatures ran and returned [Ezekiel 1:14]), and hence was the Covenant
made. . . .*

In qabalistic philosophy, there are three veils prior to existence,
Ain (Nothing), Ain Soph (The Limitless), and Ain Soph Aur (The
Limitless Light). They formulate the limitless potentialities of the
Nameless One not yet called into being. These unmanifested ideas
begin their cycle of unfoldment concentrated in the first Sephirah,
titled Kether (the Crown). Focused and located at the most inner
center of consciousness, Kether initiates all acts of creation. However at this stage no measurable dimensions of form exist. Ema-
nating directly from Kether, the second Sephirah, Chokmah (Wisdom), perfectly duplicates and reflects its essence. Father of all
consciousness, the Universal Male temporarily remains power-
less until the number three forms the Triangle of Artificiality,
which is the gateway of the abstract toward perceptibility. The
third Sephirah, Binah (Understanding), completes and makes
evident the Supernal Trinity. Co-equal in status, she is the great
productive Mother eternally in conjugal union with the Father
for the maintenance of the universe. Impregnated by Chokmah,
Binah receives and evolves the seeds of life, giving birth and form
to all creation. Revealing the resplendent glory of God to the
Blessed Ones, the Holy Shekinah embraces all the children of
light.

The fourth Sephirah, Chesed (Love), portrays the cosmic
and personal powers of memory. This anabolic function of consciousness classifies and preserves all patterns of thought and

---

*Sepher Yetzirah: The Book of Formation, translated by Wm. Wynn Westcott
(London: J.M. Watkins, 1911), pp. 15, 16.

form as they evolve in human beings and the universe. The fifth Sephirah, Geburah (Strength), is the seat of the will, creating our individuality. As the catabolic aspect of our being, its principles break down all forms that stagnate the further progress of consciousness. Therefore this Sephirah causes new channels of thought and action to emerge. The sixth Sephirah, Tiphareth (Beauty), the central sphere of the Tree, collectively receives all the powers from above, and becomes the point of their distribution to all that lies below. As the microcosmic King who wears the Crown of Kether, here, the human ego formulates and administers justice in the world of phenomena, through the Sephiroth below.

The ensuing centers of energy on the lowest levels of the Tree, constitute the component parts we define as personality. The seventh Sephirah, Netzach (Victory), depicts the unrelenting desire of the Self to bring its objectives into visible expression. The eighth Sephirah, Hod (Splendor), is the abode of the intellect, which constantly seeks and selects the ways and means to transform all arising desires into actuality. The ninth Sephirah, Yesod (Foundation), represents the automatic consciousness. Operating on the unconscious level, these habitual instinctive patterns of past evolutionary activity, structure the storehouse of the reproductive psychic energies. The tenth Sephirah, Malkuth (Kingdom), completes the cycle of the forces initiated in Kether. Their combination and fusion form the basis of all matter present in the physical world.

Of course, this general outline of the Tree of Life is solely a preliminary introduction. Complete exposition of the fundamentals of the qabalistic system would require many volumes. Further understanding may be acquired through research, study, meditation, and most important, active participation in the principles revealed.

THE PATH TO WISDOM

Throughout these chapters you have received in clear terms portions of the esoteric teachings. Now I just want to explain a little about ritual to readers who may pursue the secret teachings. Ritual is a very important factor in any mystical training. In the west, great emphasis has always been placed upon ceremonial magic and rightly so. Distinctive in the popular medieval grimoires of magical procedure is the manufacturing and consecrating of the circle, triangle, wand, chalice, sword, pentacle and other important paraphernalia required in its execution. When the magician is fully prepared, the ritual is a dramatic presentation of spoken words coupled with definite physical movements and gestures. The ritual is intended to induce temporally certain mental and chemical reactions in the body of the operator. This in turn, creates unusual atmospheric conditions in the immediate surrounding area. The objective is to evoke from the greater depths of the unconscious a selected response which under normal conditions would be impossible to reach. To a certain degree, in another manner, modern psychology operates along these lines.

In antiquity, simple ritual fulfilled the needs of primitive people. As evolution brought forth complexities in consciousness, intricate and extravagant methods of ritual celebration were introduced. However, today most of the medieval ceremonial methods are limited in scope, costly, and not very practical for the average person to undertake. Modern magicians, like our enlightened brothers and sisters of the past, are well aware that all magic begins with the discipline of the human will, and that the magical paraphernalia deemed necessary in any ceremony is actually symbolic of forces present within the consciousness of all human beings.

Knowing that its purpose is to stir the unconscious toward selected ends, new powerful methods of ritual celebration were perceived and formulated. Though its practice demands longer periods of training, and may not be as dramatic and spectacular as working with ritual, the study, meditation, and active participation in the theurgic formula of the tarot and the Tree of Life assures its initiates safe psychological and physical reactions, and most important, by incorporating its supersensory illuminations into the personality, permanent psychic and spiritual development gradually unfolds. These permanent changes are more desirable to the learned magician than temporary effects. Though you may have not been fully aware, throughout these many chapters you have been exposed to one of the most potent and cultivated forms of magic, designed to elevate sense perception to transcendental levels of existence.

Preaching both eastern and western ways, today—as in the past—there are more cults and self-proclaimed gurus than you can shake a leg at. Careful research will reveal that the majority of these seeming masters of wisdom have other motives than helping to raise the spiritual elevation of the individual. Honestly interested aspirants may fall prey to well-written advertisements or inducements promising them all and everything, only to experience disappointment as the years pass by. Much of what is taught in groups is readily available from any decent oriental or metaphysical bookshop. However, hidden within this mass of diversion is truly an Inner School of Wisdom, which continues to remain selective, exclusive, and approachable only by the fully prepared student with genuine spiritual objectives.

One of the few of its outer branches in modern times, The Hermetic Order of the Golden Dawn, unfolded during the latter part of the 19th century. A semi-private organization, its membership was composed of fewer than a hundred members, including many leading professional and talented men and women of that period. Considering the history of its activities, we unfortunately conclude that as its leaders became careless in the selection of qualified applicants, the order began to disintegrate. Egotism replaced spiritual aims, and eventually internal conflict brought about its collapse. However, in this organization's surviving manuscripts, which each member had to copy by hand, there remain recorded portions of the secret doctrine never before obtainable for public scrutiny. Their legacy of enlightenment continues to have the greatest influence upon all who find interest in the study of mystical knowledge.

Today, the availability of many instructive books written by the experienced participants makes it possible for serious students to acquire, through patience and persistent study, the essential fundamental knowledge. Once conditioned with the basics, increased discriminative powers liberate the well-informed from all that would misdirect their effects.

We look upon divination as being the least important aspect of the tarot. Our course of study is more interested in the fact that adequate understanding and application of the universal principles revealed in the tarot provides information that we can consciously use to create our future in the manner we desire, rather than depending upon questionable predictions that may insinuate conditions or situations beyond our control.

My work is completed for the moment and I dedicate this book to the Fraters and Sorores who are determined, steadfast, and in undeviating pursuit of the spiritual truth and knowledge. May the inner light of the wise rend its veil, and shower its splendors upon you.

As a very young man, Joseph D'Agostino was fascinated by the mysterious pictures of the tarot and desired to learn more about their fundamental use and meaning. He found a teacher who taught him the basics, and with this knowledge, D'Agostino explored the volumes of literature on the subject, in time discovering the universal wisdom that lay buried beneath the veiled symbolism of each card. Believing that the tarot is a powerful instrument to induce psychic as well as mystical phenomena, D'Agostino uses the cards daily; he feels that direct participation is the only way to truly understand the tarot.

Joseph D'Agostino is an accomplished musician. A graduate of Julliard, who majored in Clarinet and Composition, he went on to work with the Mascagni Opera and other classical organizations, and toured as a jazz musician throughout the United States and Europe. He lives in New Jersey and is active in the theater as a writer-composer. Currently, he is pursuing the full production of his favorite musical, "The Winds of Change," based on the life of Madame Blavatsky.